T0195712

AN INSPIRATION FROM

MIKINSON HENRY

WESTBOW
PRESS®
A DIVISION OF THOMAS NELSON
& ZONDERVAN

Scripture quotations marked NJB are from The New Jerusalem Bible, copyright © 1985 by Darton, Longman & Todd, Ltd. and Doubleday, a division of Random House, Inc. Reprinted by Permission.

Scripture quotations marked NIV are taken from the Holy Bible, New International Version®. NIV®. Copyright © 1973, 1978, 1984 by International Bible Society. Used by permission of Zondervan. All rights reserved.

Contemporary English Version® Copyright © 1995 American Bible Society. All rights reserved.

WestBow Press books may be ordered through booksellers or by contacting:

WestBow Press
A Division of Thomas Nelson & Zondervan
1663 Liberty Drive
Bloomington, IN 47403
www.westbowpress.com
1 (866) 928-1240

ISBN: 978-1-9736-0157-9 (sc)
ISBN: 978-1-9736-0158-6 (hc)
ISBN: 978-1-9736-0156-2 (e)

Library of Congress Control Number: 2017913835

Print information available on the last page.

WestBow Press rev. date: 10/20/2017

CONTENTS

ACKNOWLEDGMENTS

Reflective Readers: Rev. Patrick J. Kalich

Rev. Kevin Scalf C.PP.S.

Deacon Daniel Lowery, PhD

Sr. Sallie Latkovich, SCJ

Sr. Joanne Marie Schutz, SS.C.M.

Anthony M. Bonta, PhD

Editor and proofreader: Megan Henry

PREFACE

*T*his book is an inspiration from God. I refer to it as "the word of God," which has been given to me by God to share with his people. God spoke to me, and I listened, whether it was in my sleep, during my commutes to work, at home, or in church.

God allowed me to decipher his words and share them with you. I am not capable or worthy to write about God, but the Spirit of God is within me. Have you heard the phrase that "God can play a symphony even on a broken violin"? I am that broken violin, I am the broken instrument, I am the lost sheep that has been found by God. My existence is nowhere to be found without God. Even at my lowest, God continues to grace me with love, hope, strength, and a vision to see him in and around everything I come in contact with. I'll give everything that I have to serve God, to be with God, to love God, and to love my brothers and sisters with all my heart, mind, and soul. Sometimes, I ask this question to my Creator God: "Why haven't you given me enough wealth to rescind my struggles, to live a comfortable earthly life so that I can praise you more?" God has told me that me, "Earthly wealth is not my plan for you. My plan for you is to let my spirit lead you, to live in you, to live the life of my people so that you can better understand their struggles, which will help you to be better equipped and be more conversant with my plans and my missions." I think that is very apodictic because sometimes our struggles help to reshape ourselves to do better and to be a better person in life. It can bring a better understanding, a deeper love, and a thriving connection with God and his people. God has an unconditional and undying love for us, but we also have to be able to love our neighbors. When we can truly attain that, our glass will be full and overflowing with true love.

INTRODUCTION

My hope is that you will be enlightened by these words from God as you continue your journey to the beatific vision. May these words help you to strengthen your love for God and assist you in being a good steward in our society today, with a great mind, a good spirit, and a keen sense of discipleship. May these words help you to stay focused on God so that you can stay above the water. May God also be with you while reading his word and help you understand it in his light and presence. My hope is that this collection will inspire you and strengthen your soul's connection with God. May you always carry his Spirit within you.

WHEN SHALL YOU KNOW GOD?

When you give your whole heart to God,
then you shall know God.
When you treat every human being with
dignity and respect, then you shall
know God.

When you have a desire to read Scriptures,
follow the Tradition, and be attentive to the Magisterial teaching,
then you shall know God.
When vanity is no longer an obsession in your life, then you shall
know God.

When your heart is impervious to prejudice,
then you shall know God.
When worldly things have no meaning
to you, then you shall know God.

When God is in every aspect of your life,
then you shall know God.
When your faith is strong, even when it is tested,
then you shall know God.

When there is hope, even when you're in
distress, then you shall know God.
When you begin to know how to love,
then you shall know God.

GOD'S LOVE IS THE CYNOSURE
OF THE UNIVERSE

Without God, love is obsolete.
Without love, God cannot exist.
Without peace, love cannot breathe.

Without God, boast is infinite.
Without peace, life cannot flourish.
Without "the shepherd, the sheep"[1] cannot survive.

Without "the shepherd, the sheep" have no fame.
Without a good heart, the stream of love does not flow.
Without a good desire, love does not exist.

---

[1] Ezek 34:12 NJB

KNOWING GOD'S LAW BY LOVE

O God, they are not conversant with your law.
They do not know what's right and wrong.
The whole world is upside-down.
They do not abide by your law.

O Lord, "your kingdom is at hand."[2]
They are feeding poison to your children
to obliterate one another.
They have stoic hearts.

O God, your children are suffering on a quotidian basis.
How long will it carry on?
How long will it take to rescind this madness?

O Lord, when will they know that your law is above every other law?
When will they understand that evil is not your way?
When will they come to understand that your way is authentic and pure?

O God, when will they understand that your way is the truth?
When will they know that your way is the
ultimate route to the promised land?

O Lord, when will they have a good grasp at your law?
When will they start carrying your image?
When will they start loving each other the way you've
created them to be loved?

O God, when will hate no longer exist in this world?
When will love take over the insanity?
When will they know your way?

---

[2] Mt 3:2 NJB

LOVE

Love is not an object but a heart that needs fondness and caressing.
Love is a little child that needs nurturing.
Love is frangible when not cared for.

Love is life, and life is love.
Love is a river that flows through a good heart.
Love is what makes the world at peace.

Love is the panacea for a malicious world.
Love is light, and light is love.
Love is not just a carnal desire.

Love is great dedication, which gives us hope and certainty when it seems to be out of reach.
Love is willingness that runs through our blood stream to purify ourselves from enmity.
Love is immutable when a good heart is present.

Love is love!

STRETCH OUT YOUR HANDS

Stretch out your hands; let the moon shine.
Stretch out your hands; let the stars twinkle.
Stretch out your hands; let the birds sing.

Stretch out your hands; let the world sing.
Stretch out your hands; let the love dance.
Stretch out your hands; let your heart sing.

Stretch out your hands; let your heart be taken.
Stretch out your hands; let the sun shine.
Stretch out your hands; let heaven open wide.

UNWORTHY TO CHANGE
THE WORLD

The moon cannot replace the sun.
The sun cannot replace the moon.
The night cannot replace the day.
The day cannot replace the night.

The sky cannot replace the sea.
The sea cannot replace the sky.
The stars cannot replace the moon.
The moon cannot replace the stars.

The dead cannot replace the living.
The living cannot replace the dead.
The earth cannot replace heaven.
You cannot replace your Creator.

WHERE I SEE CHRIST'S FACE

Where I see Christ's face, heaven exists.
Where I see Christ's face, the snow falls.
Where I see Christ's face, angels sing.

Where I see Christ's face, the world rejoices.

Where I see Christ's face, everything is pure.
Where I see Christ's face, everything is perfect.
Where I see Christ's face, rain falls.

Where I see Christ's face, there is no blemish.

Where I see Christ's face, the wind blows.
Where I see Christ's face, everything is immaculate.
Where I see Christ's face, the feast begins.

Where I see Christ's face, everything is alive.

THROUGH GOD

Through God everything is true.
Through God there is no obfuscation.
Through God there is no blunder.

Through God erroneous teaching is obsolete.
Through God myopic view is an enigma.
Through God every mind is trenchant.

Through God everything is real and fruitful.
Through God everything is in harmony, like a symphony.
Through God everything is pragmatic.

GOD IS EVERYTHING

God is the love that is never-ending.
God is life that is infinite.
God is the light that is never extinguished.

God is the day that is always bright.
God is the night without darkness.
God is the one with mighty power.

God is God.

O MIGHTY

O Mighty, your power is true.

O Mighty, your love is so great.
O Mighty, your angels are blessed.
O Mighty, with you there is no limit.

O Mighty, your world is heaven.
O Mighty, with you I am blessed.
O Mighty, with you I am alive.

O Mighty, your grace is your love.

WHERE DO WE GO?

The earth has its own world.
Those with malicious intents have their own world.
Those who carry the hate in their hearts have their own world.

Tornadoes have their own world.
Avalanches have their own world.
Tsunamis have their own world.

Vanity has its own world.
Those with avaricious intents have their own world.
Those who carry the image of the world have their own world.

Destruction has its own world.
The devil has his world.
Are you ready to meet your Creator?

GOD IS THE ONE

God is the source of life that exists in a good heart.
God is the source of water that quenches every thirst.
God is the one that we need when our world seems to be in shambles.
God is the one who forgives when our world is so vindictive.

God is the source of our vision that can help us see the light.

God is the body that makes the world move.
God is the one with unconditional love for us.
God is the source of intellect that levitates our thinking.
Without God, we cannot go on, and our life would reduce to nothing.

IN GOD

In God we've found life; that life is infinite.
In God we've found love; that love is immense.
In God we've found truth; "that truth will set us free."[3]

In God we've found "passion of the cross, that passion
is an absolute gesture of his love for us."[4]
In God we've found vision; that vision is to enlighten us with the truth.
In God we've found comfort; that comfort is in our healing.

In God we've found joy; that joy is a building block and a driving
force in our lives.

[3] Jn 8:32 NJB
[4] Rom 5:8 NJB

EVERYTHING CHANGES

The world is changing.
The earth is changing.
The planets are changing.
The way of thinking is changing.
The technology is changing.
The science is changing.

The people are changing.

The minutes are changing.
The hours are changing.
The days are changing.
The nights are changing.
The months are changing.
The years are changing.

God never changes.

GOD'S LAW

God's law is above all that has existed.
God's law is supreme in the eyes of many.
God's law is our command, and we should follow it.
God's law is the mediator of our evil thinking.
God's law is what everyone should obey, in order to live in peace.
God's law is what everyone should follow, every single day.

God's law is the gate of truth and the paradise of knowledge.

God's law is ever-present for those who have it in their hearts.
God's law is what everyone should strive for, in order to find success.
God's law is a gift for every person that follows and observes the truth.
God's law is here to stay, and so is his company.
God's law is the divine one that comes from heaven.
God's law is more precious than anything on earth.

God's law will set us free.

SEARCHING

Searching for your truth when I am lost.
Searching for the answer when no one has it but you.
Searching for guidance when no one can guide but you.
Searching for the way when I don't know where to go.
Searching for love when it seems to be lost.
Searching for peace when there seems to be none.

Searching to decipher what I cannot comprehend.

Searching for a leader when no one can lead but you.
Searching for the light when it seems to be far away.
Searching for a way out when you're the only egress.
Searching for heaven when it seems to be out of reach.
Searching for wisdom that seems to be ignored.
Searching for food where yours is the only one that is real.

Searching for life, but Christ is the only source of it.

OBSTINACY

Why are you so obstinate to hear the good news?
Do you not know that Christ's words are divine and more precious
than anything in this world?
Do you not know that Christ is our Savior and his words can "set you
free?"[5]
Do you not know that Christ is the King of all?
and he rules the world with his might?

Do you not know that Christ's power has no limit
and stretches throughout the world?
Do you not know that Christ's grace flows throughout the world
and reaches every single one of his Father's creatures?
Do you not know that Christ is unequivocally the answer
for everything obscure?

Do you not know that "Christ is the Alpha and the Omega?"[6]

---

[5] Jn 8:32 NJB
[6] Rev 22:13 NJB

WHEN I GET TO SEE GOD

When I get to see God, my heart will be at peace.
When I get to see God, there will be no distress.
When I get to see God, my face will be brand-new.
When I get to see God, my whole world will change.

When I get to see God, I won't stop smiling.
When I get to see God, there will be no death.
When I get to see God, I will be cured and pure.
When I get to see you, my sins will no longer exist.

When I get to see God, I will make you proud.
When I get to see God, heaven will smile.
When I get to see God, I will be a member of his choir.
When I get to see God, my life will be eternal.

EVERYTHING CAME FROM GOD

Inspiration came from God.
All the great philosophical thinking came from God.
All the great improvisations came from God.
Gifted minds came from God.

Apodictic way of thinking is God's nature.
A clean heart came from God.
Motivation to strive came from God.
All of the great intellect came from God.

Mediocrity is not God's way; it's the devil.

YOUR HEART IS NOT THERE

How can you love when your heart is outside his body?
How can you smile when your smile is strikingly factitious?
How can you change the world when your intentions are elsewhere?

How can you construct when you aim at destruction?
How can the blind lead the blind?
How can you share your wealth when your wealth is your temple?

How can you change your way of living when you are extremely obstinate at everything that is divine?
How can one see love in you when you have a stony heart?
How can you make a difference in the world when you separate yourself from what can lead you to him?

How can your Father be proud when you are having dinner with the devil?
How can the sea stay calm when your heart is quarrelsome?
How can we have unity when your heart and every angle of your brain are divisive?

You are in no-man's-land. God is the only one who can save you!

PRETENDERS

They pretend to be real, but deep inside their hearts
they are "two-edged swords."[7]
They pretend to be true disciples of their Savior, but they are not
following his law.
They pretend to show love to their neighbors, but inside their hearts
is all rotten with hate.
They pretend to tell the truth, but they are deceitful.

They pretend to be your great guest, but they are destroying your temple.
They pretend to be evangelizers, but inside they are empty.
They pretend to smile, but their smiles are factitious.

They pretend to tell the truth, but their truth has no ground.
They pretend to show unity, but inside they are divisive.
They pretend to be true intellects, but they don't know what is right
and wrong.
They pretend to know authentic science, but they don't know it came
from him.

They pretend to know it all, but they don't accept your teachings.
They pretend to do philanthropic works, but they are ignoring the
needs of the poor and they are taking everything that is supposed to
go to the poor.
They pretend serve the poor, but they are vilifying them at every
angle and in every opportunity that they get.
They do everything backward and awkwardly, but I am not the judge;
our Lord is.

---

[7] Heb 4:12 NJB

OBSCURITY

The ocean seems to be still, but it's not.
The moon seems to be near, but it's not.
The clouds seem to be at a proximity, but they're not.
The sky seems to be blue, but it's not.

The lies of the devil seem to be true, but they are not.
Black holes seem to be small, but they're not.
The cobra seems to be in a deep sleep, but it's not.
Stay vigilant, keep your optical views open,
so that you aren't deceived by the deceitful angels.

CHRIST IS EVERYTHING
THAT IS GOOD

Can't you see that "Christ is the vine and you are the branches"?[8]

Christ is the temple, and you are his worshippers.
Christ is the way, and you are his followers.
Christ is the teacher, and you are his students.

Christ is the law, and you are his witnesses.
Christ is the life, and you are his receivers.
Christ is the Son, and you are his brothers and sisters.

Christ is the Savior, and you are his people.

[8] Jn 15:5 NIV

CONFUSION

My thoughts are traveling at the speed of light,
with so many ideas but little guidance.
I live in a world where pensivity is the norm.
Where can I rest my conception? I am a neophyte who is
in the chrysalis stage.

Trying to decipher the unknown in this esoteric world.
I am trying to find the ultimate route, where I can rest my thoughts
and visions.
Sometimes I wonder if my world could be better, but I am divagating
because I am where God wants me to be.

BIG DREAMS

Big dreams come with hard work, innovation, admiration,
and an excellent vision that can change the world.
Great dedication and willingness can assure us that the route is not
nebulous.
When a cohesive heart collides with a sagacious mind, it can spark
greatness,
which can assure us that there is no dichotomy between a great mind
and a great heart.

They are analogous in every aspect and every angle in which our
mind allows us to decipher those dreams.
Everyone has big dreams and wants to put a final touch on them, but
they are not on a silver platter.

God needs to be in your plan so that you can prosper.

EVERYTHING DEPENDS
ON SOMETHING

Fruits do not produce without trees, because they need their maker to be conducive.

A violin does not have the capacity to play a symphony without its great player, the same way the player cannot be a virtuoso without a brain.

Without great teachers and students, classes would not be in existence.

It is in the same manner that the Church cannot exist without its priests.

Plants cannot grow without photosynthesis and water.

Beautiful-looking hospitals cannot give great care without great doctors.

Your life would not come into play if your Creator did not exist.

Great fields cannot produce great scores without great players.

It is the same way that great homilies cannot come into existence without great priests and deacons.

It would be impossible to live forever without the bread that is divine.

Emancipate your mind and help it to come to a conclusion that your Creator needs you to strengthen his kingdom.

ONCE YOU COME TO KNOW GOD

Once you come to know God, you will begin to love and change every aspect of your life.

You will begin to catch things that are uncatchable by others.

Unless you are a part of that mystical body, you will not be conversant with it.

Your heart will be touched by God; it will be cleansed and pure.

Your mind will be fixed on God like a covalent bond that brings you to the Spirit of the Trinity, knowing that he is the ultimate Savior.

Your action will be flawless, unequivocally noticed by others, and they will begin to see that your heart is in God.

Your heart will be fixed on God like a magnet, and you will know that your eschatological needs depend not only on God but also on your own self.

Once you come to know God, the moon will bow down.

IDOLATRY

Why are you worshipping everything in this world that has no value and cannot save you?

Don't you know that you need to worship the true and divine one? The one who gives you free will and intellect, the one who does not want you to fall into the darkness.

Can't you see that you're abusing your own free will? You're alienating yourself from your Creator. On the contrary, free will should give you the freedom to worship him anywhere, any place, and anytime, without limits.

How long will you know that his kingdom is not a place you can buy your way into?

How long will it take to come to grips that doing your Father's work should be the priority?

When will you have a concrete plan of meeting your Creator's will?

When will you realize the dark side is not where your Father wants you to be?

When will you understand the kingdom of your ultimate Savior?

SO MANY DO NOT KNOW

There are so many who ignored your law, so many in quandaries and situations who do not know where to go.
They can't seem to understand that your way is the way.
There is no contrition inside their hearts, Lord. Show them the way!

O Lord, teach them wisdom, help them to understand. Show them the diacritical aspects of your law because your law is pure and it knows good and evil.
In your law, there are no worries, no trespasses, no myopic views, no errors, no contretemps.
Everything is as perfect as it should be.

Lord, help them to understand that your law can pave the way for them, your law can set them free in a way that can produce eternal happiness.
Your law is what separates you from the pretenders. Your law is what is good for every one of your children.
Your law is the ultimate ticket to heaven, where we and the Paraclete can praise you eternally.

SO UNGRATEFUL

Father, I am so ungrateful to know your unconditional love for me, so unworthy to be your child and your servant.

I can't seem to be conversant with all the things that you went through for me, your tribulations and shameful death, just to save our race.

You're always there for me when I am in sorrow, when I need comfort and spiritual help.

Sometimes I feel like I don't exist, but you've elevated me to the dignity of a human being.

When my world seems like it's going to crash, you're always there for me.

How can I repay you, my Lord, and have a better understanding of your law?

BETTER UNDERSTANDING
OF YOUR MAKER

Some say, why do I have to talk about you all the time?
Why are they so obstinate to talk about you?
They can talk about everything else that is negligent, but they feel so
lethargic, so jaded to talk about their ultimate Savior.
Can they tell me who is better to talk about than you?

Can they tell me the reason why they exist in this world?
When I hear people say that I talk about Christ too much, it rips my
heart apart to see a man who gave his life and died on the cross for
us and we grow tired of talking about him.
What kind world are we living in? Are we in a crisis?
Can we have a better understanding of you, my Lord, and not be
afraid or too tired to talk about you on a continual basis?

STAY FOCUSED

Better effort can lead to more open doors than you knew existed.
Ambition to strive may make your future brighter.
Hard work can pay off in the short and in the long run.

Staying adroit at everything that you do can facilitate your way of living.
Stay focused, be the brightest that you can be in every aspect of your life.
Always do the best you can in whatever task you are taking on because your effort will not be in vain.

Feed your body with all the good things because an empty sac cannot stand on its own, nor an empty stomach or spirit and soul.

STAY POSITIVE

Some say, how can we pray to a God that we cannot see?
How can we love our neighbors when they don't have the same desire?
How can we see him in every single creature, even those led by evil?

How can we stay satiable when the world is so avaricious?
How can we give when others cling to their own?
How can we save the world when others are destroying it?

How can we teach when others don't want to learn?
Look around. He is everywhere, in every heart, every smile, and everything that is good.
Don't be gullible to those erroneous teachings; look for God. You will see the light.

MOTHERS

Mothers are the most beautiful things in the world, and the greatest human being to ever put feet on earth is a mother, "our Blessed Mother."[9]

Without mothers in the world, we would not come to be.

Mothers are what make the world move; without their love, care, and nurturing, the world would come to an end.

I am trying to find the words that can describe them, but too many come to mind.

A library would be too small to hold the word "mothers"; it would take the world to write about them.

Mothers are incomparable, better than gold, silver, diamonds, and all the precious things in this world.

When I see mothers, I see love, life, and happiness that is infinite.

Mothers! How can I pay you back for showing me the world?

I can't seem to find the words that describe you and the rewards on this earth that are suitable for you because none of these things in the world are enough to compensate you but heaven.

[9] Lk 1:42 NJB

PRINCE OF PEACE

"Prince of Peace"![10] Bring tranquility to this madness.
Pour out the living water to this uncanny world that we live in,
where lies, fallacious accusations, insult, disrespectful manner,
and destroying lives are the precedent.

Prince of the universe, let the "river of peace flow"[11] into the hearts
of your children.
Renew their faiths and their hearts because it is killing inside those
who follow your precepts and your law.
I feel like a fainéant human being sometimes when I see that I cannot
bring much peace to this crazy world, but I leave it up to you.

"Prince of Peace," cleanse their hearts with love and bring water into
their wine.

---

[10] Isa 9:5 NJB
[11] Isa 66:12 NJB

GIVE YOUR HEART TO GOD

Spread the faith and let love flow.
See God in every person and every living creature.
Bring love to everything that God created.
Embellish his word with his own Spirit.

Show Christ the love that he shows to you on the cross.
Give Christ your heart, and he'll renew your soul.
His soul, his heart, his mind, and body are Christocentric, and
so is his love.

Living on this earth is transitory, but our lives can be eternal
if we follow the right path that will lead us to God.

IF YOU HAD YOUR WAY

Vanity is worthless, and so is a lame mind.
The world is a mess, and so is the flesh of the body.
If your evil mind had its way, the world would be extinct.
There would be no heaven but you and hell.

Great attribution and the love of God would not come into play.
You ought to hurry because the train is leaving,
and the time is now to get to know God.

BE ATTENTIVE

Don't be so refractory! Listen to the "Priest,"[12] "Prophet,"[13] and "King."[14]
Listen to him because his words are divine, true, and alive.
His law is the ultimate and the only legitimate one.

His law is above all that have existed in the universe.
He's the light that is never extinguished and beyond compare.
His love never ends, nor his grace.

Be attentive! Because Jesus Christ is your only Savior, and everything else is worthless.

---

[12] Heb 2:17 NJB
[13] Mt 21:11 NJB
[14] Rev 1:5 NJB

COME, JESUS

Come cure a heart that is full of malignancy and broken in pieces.
Help save a soul that is lost and a mind that doesn't recognize its body.
Help me see the light that you have created to illumine the minds of
your children.

Open my eyes because I am blind and help me fight
a battle that is so fierce because I am feeble and jaded.
Saturate my mind with intellect and all the goodness that exists.
Come and fill a glass that is empty and mind that has paucity of
knowledge, because you have it, and you can make me bright like a star.

Come and help rescue this itinerant man who has no place to stay.
Come and help me fight these pugnacious enemies because I cannot
do it on my own.
Come help a poor and needy man who does not have a clue.

HEAVEN

Heaven is whiter than snow, and its garden is greener than green.
Beautiful angels are everywhere and surround in the air like wings
of messengers.
In this beautiful heaven, seraphim lead the choir. There
is no hate but love, no sin but purity, no lies but truths.

Heaven, where all adore the King of the universe.

In heaven, where there is no nonsense but knowledge and truth.
O beautiful heaven, when I think of you, I feel so ebullient, and
my heart won't stop singing.
O precious heaven, you give me hope when there is none and
make me see what lies ahead of me.

O sweet heaven, where cherubim bear the throne of your King and
stand at the gate to welcome your newest members.
You fix a heart that was broken in piece and beyond repair.
O precious heaven, you've renewed a faith that was lost.

FOLLOW THE PATH THAT
LEADS YOU TO GOD

A triangle has three sides, but it's one, so as the Trinity and divinity. Your brain gives you the ability to think and retain what you have learned, which makes you who you are.

Three persons with three different aspects, but in this body, there is cohesiveness, divinity, and unity, with an undefiled and an undivided law that unifies that body.

You see what your eyes want you to see,
and you hear what your ears want you to hear.
You think what your brain wants you to think,
and you eat what your taste wants you to eat.
You touch what your hands want you to touch.

Can you pause for a minute to listen to the good news?
Can you do what your savior wants you to do? To follow his law
and his command that is written in your heart.
Would you give him "your whole heart, mind, body, and soul?"[15]

Attentiveness needs to be your norm, so that you can be steadfast. Don't let the master of all deceit make you think otherwise and separate you from the divine law, which is all that you need.

Don't be so gullible to those unscrupulous behaviors.

Thoroughly examine your conscience, and you will know the truth, which will convert you to a new human being and a child of your Savior.

---

[15] Lk 10:27 NJB

MAKE ME YOUR CHILD AGAIN, LORD

Restore the life in me that is a mess.
Bring to life this itinerant soul.
Restore a heart that is troublesome and
bring peace to this pugnacious mind.

Come and cure this disease inside of me.
If there is light after this tunnel, then my hope
is still alive, and my heart will be cured and pure.
I will see you in every human, in every single human being.

I will "love my neighbors as myself,"[16] and I will forget and forgive
those who hurt me.
I will have a deep contrition for sin, and then I will
be a child again.

---

[16] Mk 12:31 NJB

SOMETIMES WHAT WE SEE DOES NOT SUBSIST IN THE TRUTH

The grass might look greener on the other side, but don't let that fool you.
The box might look more beautiful, more precious than anything else on the outside.
Don't let your mind be deceived.
All the things that seem to be beautiful on the outside are not what they look on the inside, with an exception of divinity.

A real genius will not mention how acute his mind is, but others will.
Be cautious, for what you view as treasure, may be a deception in fact.
Don't let this world fool you because your gold mine is right here with you.
Open up your eyes so that you can see the light.

STAY PEACEFUL

The beauty on the inside is even more beautiful than the one on the outside.
Give life a chance to breathe and love time to embellish its beauty.
Calm your ocean that is enraged.

Why so morose when you can be at peace?
Why hate when you can love and there is no string attached to it?
Why sit down crossing your arms and legs when you can help others who are in need?
Why is your world in turmoil when it can be at rest?
Can you tell him why your mind is so sporadic when it can be fixed on the prize?

Why so peevish when everyone around has much love for you?
I am not trying to judge the law; instead I am observing it.
Or maybe it's my conjecture that you need a little structure in your nature so that it can compensate for your future.

Don't be so capricious. Put an end to your madness and calm your saturnine world.
Let the river flow peacefully to your brain and your world.
Let the world see the light and new life in you and
what your Master has in store for you.

BE A GOOD STEWARD

Can you love with your whole heart and speak with your whole mind?
Can you go above and beyond for the one you love to make your
Father proud?
Would you have the same attitude and approach toward a stranger?
Can you bear insults for the sake of peace and love?

Can you be exemplary in every aspect of your life,
for those who have trust in you and the law?
Can you make the world see him in you, in your working progress?
Can you change the lives of many by your speech and conduct?

Can your charisma be originated from another source?

BE ACTIVE AND DON'T WASTE TIME

Your time is now. What must you do to give honor and glory to your Lord? What must you do now to give your whole heart to him?

What must you do in order to prepare yourself for the beatific vision? What must you do to be a catalyst of the missions of your Savior?

You must seize the occasion and come in accordance with that natural law, which is written in your heart.
Don't be a bystander; action matters.

What must you do to come to reality and search what is good for your mind, body, and soul?

Give your whole heart to God so that you can be prepared to meet him. Let nothing separate you and distract you from the teaching of Christ. Be very acute at what you do.

WHO IS HE?

Who is your God?
The one who always forgives you every time that you sin.

Who is your Master?
The one who cares for you more than anyone and anything
in the world.

Who is your caregiver and your caretaker?
The one who is always taking care of you and rescues you
whenever you're falling off the cliff.

Who shows you love in a quotidian basis?
The one who has infinite and unconditional love for you.

Who is your Redeemer?
The one who died on the cross for you
in order to save you and expiate your sins.

How can you pay him back? "Love your neighbors as yourself."[17]
Love every single living thing that he has created. Do his work.
Love him for the sake of his love for you.

That way you can be recognized not only by your brothers and sister
but also by your Holy Father.

---

[17] Mt 22:39 NJB

47

LIFE

Life begins with love, and love begins with life.
Love begins with care, and care transcends to life.
Wisdom is essential when carrying the cross of our Lord.

Intellect is a must when preaching the Word of God.
Willingness is the catalyst of the heart that never stops beating.
Abnormality is not the norm in his house.

Perseverance is a force that leads you to many accolades.
A great vision can enlighten and change the mind of many.
A great mind with kindness can also open the eyes of many.

Trust and respect can bring life to a new level of understanding.
Life can only flourish if you give it a chance.
You can only prosper if you allow it to flow through "your heart, mind, and soul."[18]

---

[18] Lk 10:27 NJB

STRUGGLE

Sometimes I wonder why I struggle in life so much.
Struggle to pay bills and struggle to take care of this beautiful family
that I have.
Struggle to follow your law and struggle to be like you.
Struggle to take care of my everyday obligation.

Lord, I have to ask you, why do I have to face all these difficulties,
even in the path of my lay ministry classes, struggling to take care of
the payment for these classes?
I have encountered so many obstacles that I cannot even count. Then
I ask you, why do I have to go to all these difficulties?

Your response is, "So that you can live in the presence of me and you
can know my way.
I want you to look at the cross, live my life in time of suffering so
that you can know how to lead my people in a better way when the
opportunities come.
In order for you to be conversant with my teaching to know me better,
you have to struggle, so that you can know the struggle of my people.
You have to suffer so that you can know the suffering of my people.

"I have to live in you, so that you can live in me and you'll know the
living presence of my law.
When you suffer, your life is united with me; you live in the moment
of what I went through for you, in order to save you and the world.

"It's not a matter of education; you have enough education to strive,
to drive some of the fastest cars, to have some of the most beautiful
houses on earth, but this is not my plan for you. Earthly thing is not
my way. My plan for you is to lead my people to the land of the living
in a more beautiful way.

"My way is not a way of pride; it's not a way of inferiority complex; it's not a way of showing off; it's not a way of living in this fantasy world. My way is to carry me in your heart wherever you go; my way is to have a good moral judgment; my way is to do what is acceptable to my people so that I can lead you to a more beautiful life than you can ever imagine.

"Your duty is to make my presence seen in every single thing that you do in life, to love your neighbors and respect the lives that I have created, love your brothers and sister, respect others and respect my law, so that one day you might get a chance to see me, you might get a chance to sing with my choir, you might get a chance to receive the greatest accolade that can possibly exist
for you."

YOU GIVE ME HOPE

When I see the veneration of the saints, it gives me hope, hope that I can be the next one in line.

When I live this beautiful memory on earth, it gives me hope, hope that I'll have a chance of meeting you one day.

When I see the stars at night, they give me hope, hope that I'll have a chance of sharing your love with the angels and saints in a more beautiful way that I can fathom.

It helps me to have a better understanding of my Father and helps me to choose the right path and the ultimate route.

When I see all of your goodness in the world, it lets me know that you will lead me to that beatific vision.

When I see your handiwork, it gives me hope, hope that when I leave this earth, there is a life after death.

When I see your face, it tells me that God is merciful.

It tells me that if I follow that natural law and stay close to him, that I have a chance of getting into heaven to be with my Father to sing and praise him for all eternity.

YOUR WORLD CAN BE CHANGED BY GOD FOR BETTER

God can make you look great even when you are not at your best.
If God can play a symphony on a broken instrument like me, he can
certainly play a symphony on any other broken body anywhere, at any
place and at any given day and time.

I was broken and confused, perhaps misguided by this failing society
that does not know who God is, that does not know what is right
and wrong.
We live in a society today that does not know the obligation of every
single human being that has existed in this planet Earth.
Brothers and sisters, it's time for us to acknowledge the truth and
nothing but the truth in order to save ourselves, others, and the world.

We live in a world today where one does not know where to begin
and where to finish.
Today, I encourage you, brothers and sisters, to bring Christ into your
lives, to bring Christ in every single thing that you do, which can
emancipate "your heart, mind, body, soul, and strength,"[19] so that you
may be called the children of God by your actions.
The way you carry yourself and the image of God in your heart will
make you beautiful not only in the inside but on the outside as well.

God's message to you all is to listen to him and always do what is right
in the eyes of God so that your soul won't be wasted. In following your
Lord, your God, your soul can be in more perfect harmony and be
united with Christ in your life.

---

[19] Lk 10:27 NJB

DON'T TURN YOUR BACK ON GOD

What must you do to be in accordance with that natural law?
You must stay away from sin and carry that love in your heart.
You must acknowledge the truth that is given to you by God through Scripture, Tradition, and Magisterial teaching.

You should never do anything that would put you in conflict with your Father!
You should always be a paragon to our society; you should be that person people look to for advice.
You should always show love to everyone, the one who loves you and even the one who hates you, which is what our Father taught us.

You should never disrespect your brothers and sister because that is what you're being called to do, to respect everything that God created around you.
You who are being call by God to help his people, don't step away from that teaching.
The verdict starts with you because if you're just a perfunctory ministry, it is not going to cut it, and you're not going to please God that way.

By not respecting your fellow brothers and sisters, you're separating yourself from the teaching of Christ.
If you're not observing his law, you will fall down higher from the sky. Why? Because you should know better, you the one he has chosen to pass the message to his people. To further say, Scripture said that, "The one who did not know, but has acted in such a way that he deserves a beating, will be given fewer strokes. When someone is given a great deal, a great deal will be demanded of that person; when someone is entrusted with a great deal, of that person even more will be expected."[20]
So you should do what is expected of you, not the bare minimum.

---

[20] Lk 12:48 NJB

Clothe yourself with good things because God has chosen you for a reason; don't waste that time. Make the best of it.

Be what your Lord your God called you to be: be the one who loves, be the one who is not subterfuge to your neighbor, be the one who lives by the law. Don't just carry the name Christian; actions matter. Show it to God and to your neighbors and others, in your speech and conduct and in your heart. So that way, you can make your Father proud of the time he has invested in you.

YOU MUST KNOW CHRIST

You must see the power of your Savior and the lightning of love given to us by Christ.
You must hear the thunder of loving and caring that came from Christ.
You must know that Christ is the one who has all the power.

You can show the love that Christ gives you to your society and every single thing around you.

You must love all the beautiful things that his Father has created.
You must see Christ's love in yourself and others.
You must give yourself and your whole heart to him.

Let Christ see that his investment in you is not in vain.
And it's more beautiful than you can imagine.

Let's not reject Christ's love for you; pass it on to others.
Let Christ see that his work is into perfection.
Let Christ see that you are his loving children.

FOLLOW HIS LEAD

Everything that you approach, approach it according to God's law.

The life that you see, respect it for the love of God.
The knowledge that you've been given, take it for more doors to be opened for you.
The prudence that God gives, use it for the safety of your own and others.

Everything that you touch, touch it through the hand of God.

The kindness and caring that God has shown you, pass it on to others.
The freewill that God gives you, don't let the devil make you violate it.
Don't let the devil make you abuse this precious faculty, your soul.

Every good deed that you do, do it for the love of God.

Follow your God. Don't let the devil lead you through darkness.
Everything that you do, do it according to God's law.
Everything you see, see it through the eyes of God.

Every love that you show and give, do it for the sake of God.

COME TO HIM

Take a good look at Christ on the cross and tell me that he doesn't love you.
Look at the humiliation that he went through just to save your race.
Tell me it was not for you and your brothers and sisters.
Take a look at the nails on Christ's body and tell me that his sacrifice is not sufficient for you to see the light.

Look at Christ stretching out his arms on the cross and spilling his own blood for you and tell me that you don't love him as well as your children and neighbors.
Tell me that his love for you is not unparalleled to what anyone else can give you.
It's time for you to wake up, to stop living in a bubble. It's time for you stop playing backyard music with the devil.

It's time for you to come and play in a real band, the greatest orchestra that has ever existed, the orchestra of your Lord, your God, "Jesus, the Christ."[21]
What more can Christ do to show his love for you? How much more can he do for you,
in order to accept him as your Savior?

Don't picture the world that you live in as your own world but God's world. Come to Christ, love Christ, love your brothers and sisters, and thank him for what he has done for you.
Thank your Lord for what he has done in order to save you and the whole human race.

---

[21] 1Tim 2:5 NJB

TO BE SO OBSTINATE

Don't be so tacit when it comes to telling the truth,
because only the truth can set you free from any trap that the devil
has for you,
and don't listen to those erroneous teachings either that can lead you
in the wrong direction.
See the devil try to swindle you and trick you.

Don't be so malleable; stay outside of that periphery so that you don't
get fooled by the master of all deceit.
You are shrewd enough to not fall into that trap that the devil has
prepared for you.
Don't be so complacent, change your way, change your life, change
the way you see things, change the way that you approach things, see
everything through the eyes of God.
Stay away from anything that is negative and eccentric.

Let God's foliage of love fall over your head.
Let God lead you to the right path; let him show you the way.
Let God be your teacher, your mentor, your problem solver.

Allow your Father to manifest the perfection of fatherhood.
Show God that you love him as much he loves you.
Trust God and only God because in him, your trust is surely not in vain.

HIS PROTECTION IS LIKE A ROCK

Myriads of armies approaching me to destroy me,
but they cannot touch me because my Lord is with me.
My Lord holds me like a little dove in the palm of his hands to shield
me from any attack of my enemy.

Devil is continually trying to excoriate and annihilate me,
but they have fallen. They can never get near me because my Lord
is with me.
I am millions of miles away from dangers because the mighty power
is with me all day long.

Nothing can trap me because the power of God is with me; my "heart,
mind, body, and soul"[22] are in the nest of the holy angels.
My Lord's power will protect me from any danger and anything that
is unclean and impure.

His protection for me is implacable, impervious to any danger that
would come my way.
I put my trust in the Lord always because he is my Savior, my Lord,
my God.
My Lord's protection for me is beyond compare, and his power is infinite.

---

[22] Lk 10:27 NJB

THE WAY YOU LIVE IN CHRIST

You live in Christ by carrying his cross and loving your brothers and sisters.
You live in Christ by being able to bear insults without resentment.
You live in Christ by carrying his love in your heart.

You live in Christ by admiring and loving everything his Father has created
and everything that he has instituted himself.
You live in Christ by having a good heart and faith and soul, by being conversant with the Church doctrine and being able to pass the good news to others.

You live in Christ when you've transformed to a new person, a person of Christ.
You live in Christ when you have no anger inside of you.
You live in Christ when your mood does not go with the wind.
You live in Christ when you have the capacity and the ability to listen to others.

You live in Christ when everything around you seems to work in accordance with that divine teaching.
You live in Christ when you can manifest the perfection of his law.
You live in Christ when you see nothing but him in everything that you touch.
You live in Christ when he is absolutely your ultimate Savior.

THE LOVE OF GOD

The love of God is like a snowflake.
It's like pouring rain falling down from the sky
with abundance and great power.
With God, paucity of love does not exist.

It's like pure and living water that will quench your thirst forever.
God love flows throughout the world, touching every single one of
his creatures.
It's like the cloud moving in harmony and in a synchronized way to
show us his love for us.
His eyes are fixing on his children to protect them wherever they go.

God's hands are tender to hold us and to give us comfort when are
in a deep blue sea.
His love for you is immeasurable; love him back.
Show your brothers and sisters the same love that God is showing to
you every single day.

STAY STEADFAST

Be ready and stay focused on God like a magnet because he is around the corner.

Do everything in a manner that will lead you to him.

The clock is ticking. Do not waste any more time. Hurry!

Christ is near. He will come to rule the world with great power and might.

Those who follow his law will receive great honor.

Those who follow his teaching will be with him and live forever.

And those who do not abide by his law will see

and go through that unquenchable fire.

Those who do not follow his law will go in flames.

The flames will be so immense, so elephantine, they will cover the whole earth.

It will be so high that it will reach the clouds. Those with Christ will climb that ladder to reach heaven, and those with no heart will be fried like roasts in the furnace.

Come to him, observe his law, do what is right, and do what is acceptable to him.

Leave all the unworthy behind and stop worshipping the devil.

Stop worshipping useless and unworthy gods that cannot save you.

Come to your God, your Lord Jesus Christ.

Come to your Savior, Jesus Christ. His arms are open to embrace you.

Leave all your nonsense behind and come to meet your Savior, Jesus Christ.

11/23/15 at 3:00 a.m.

STAY ALERT

Be vigilant, stay alert because Satan is on the attack mode on our Church, trying to destroy our Church, dispersing our priests and clergies, driving some of our finest priests and clergies out of our Church like smoke.

Satan dresses like a clergy wearing a black robe with a red hat.

I urge you to pray more and more and more on a quotidian basis to drive the beast out of our Church.

We know that God is the ultimate Savior and can stop the beast at any time, but we can also help our Church to stay clean and help our Lord to destroy the enemy of humanity and those who "God has created in his own image."[23]

Pray for the priests and clergies who've been driven out of the Church by Satan.

Pray for those who are in the Church, administering God's Church and his forgiveness to give them strength so that they can stay clean, strong, and focused in order to sustain the attack of the devil.

Yes, God will put an end to this madness, but we cannot stay with our arms crossed and be bystanders. Let us be part of the action in fighting the devil.

---

[23] Gen 1:27 NJB

THERE IS NOTHING
GOOD IN THE DEVIL

When your heart is full with anger, it is not you; it's the devil that is in your heart.

When you have a desiccated mind, it's not you; it's the devil's prayer in your mind.

When you can't seem to do anything right and you can't find a solution to your problem,

it's not you; it's the devil's control.

When you can't seem to be led in the right direction, it's not you; it's the devil.

When you are not making the right decision, it's not you; it's the devil.

When nothing seems to be working for you, it's not you; it's the devil.

When you feel down like you are a total failure, it's not you; it's the devil.

When you feel that there is no help coming your way, it's not you; it's the devil.

When the whole world is against you, it's not you; it's the devil.

When you can't seem to stay focused and think right, it's the devil.

When your world seems to come to an end, it's not you; it's the devil.

Save yourself, keep your eyes open, and focus on God because with him there are no worries.

YOU CAN CARRY GOD'S IMAGE

If "God created you in His own image,"[24] then you can possibly do good.

You can do good in many ways if you follow God's teaching.

You can do good to portray his image, you can do good to show that you have some similarity with your Savior.

You can show some similarities by loving one another.

You can show similarities by observing his law and his commandments.

You can show that his work is not in vain and there is hope.

You can show that God's love is still flourishing in you by doing what is right and acceptable to him.

You can show that his love and power are manifested in you.

You can show the world that he's your God and "there is no other like him."[25]

---

[24] Wis 1:23 NJB
[25] Isa 45:5 NJB

HIS LAW DOES NOT DISAPPOINT

"Put your trust in God"[26] and only God, the Most High.

If you want to be saved, follow God's law and his precepts. Don't let the devil have the upper hand over your destiny.

Your "Father's house"[27] is where you should envision to be, and that is what you should strive for.

Do not let the devil lead you to that bottom pit where there is nothing but fierce fire.

The devil cannot save you, nor can the devil lead you to the promised land.

The devil instead will lead you to the hell of the damned.

Turn yourself to God, your Savior. Give up your worldly lifestyle and live the life that God wants you to live, the life that will lead you to him.

Stay within that boundary that will unify you with Christ. Stay in that periphery; see yourself as a future saint.

Now is the time to change yourself into a great person. Now it's time to save yourself and others around you.

The almighty God will come with his great power, and those who follow his law will see the bright lights, the moon, and the stars at their "Father's house," and those who don't follow the precepts of his law, you will reduce to ashes.

---

[26] Ps 37:3 NJB
[27] Jn 14:2 NJB

DO NOT USE EXCUSES

Just because you're struggling, don't take that as an ostensible reason to question and to walk away from your Creator.

Just remember that your struggles and sufferings are wrapped up in the sufferings of Christ on the cross.

And Christ suffered even more at this moment. His precepts, his heart is saddened when we don't follow his law.

With all the killing, all the anger, all the hatred going on in this world, some have no respect for humanity

and sometimes take pleasure in destroying lives as if human beings were some kind of hunting game or targets for shooting ranges.

There will be a time that you'll have to answer your Father about your shooting sprees. There will be a time that you'll have to answer your God about those lives that you have destroyed.

Do you not have any respect for your life, and that is why you don't respect the lives of others?

Are you not in your right mind, or is the devil taking over you?

Just remember that none of you have the right to destroy lives that you didn't create because you are not the Creator.

You have created nothing authentic in this world; all the good that you see in this world is all God's creation.

You are here, in this world, because of the mercy of a great God who loves you to death.

Don't be so foolish. Put your weapons down. Think twice before you pull the trigger and destroy a human life that you did not create. Think about the ramifications of the action you're about to take.

Think of your Father, your God, your Lord and do what is right in the eyes of your Father.

FOLLOW HIS PRECEPTS

God is so caring that he gives his precious love to us.
God is so dexterous that he created the world out of nothing.
God is so merciful that he forgives us every time we sin.

God is so adept that he gave us a beautiful law to follow.
Don't think that following his law is some kind of arduous task for
you to do; just remember that his law is love, life, hope, and so facile
to follow: it's like drinking water.

In his law, there are no worries about the future, no regrets, no
nostalgia, no foolishness, no pain but all gain.
In his law, there are more accolades than you can ever think of.

You seem kind of lost sometimes. Stay steadfast and focus on the prize
that is ahead of you.
Don't let the devil vacillate your mind, trying to confuse you, trying
to make you forget your own God. Don't fall into that trap.

Listen to your Master, your God, your Lord at all times!

PRAISE HIM

Believe in God, and everything will be unequivocally pure through your eyes.
Believe in God, and you will have a bright mind.
Trust in God; your faith will not go in vain.

Praise God, and one day you will be praised by his angels and saints.
Love God and your fellow citizens, and you will be loved by his noble company.
Elucidate your acts. Come to your Father who loves you so much that he sent his only son to carry the cross for you.

Praise God, the sky will kiss the earth, and your earth will meet heaven.
West will embrace the east, and south will follow north in a timely manner.
Praise God all that you can; the wind will freely blow, and the breeze will caress the air.

Forget the things that are negligible in life and admire those that are important.
Forget and forgive those who hurt you and help bring new life into your world and theirs.
Praise God until the rainbow kisses the river and find its rest on earth.

Praise God for eternity for he is good and the God of all.
Believe in God, and nothing will be incredulous to you and impossible to accomplish.
Praise God in every single thing that you do. Praise him in the morning, at midday, and in the evening.
Give God praise in every opportunity and possibility that you get.

Praise God like you have never done before. Pay him his due for his love is infinite.
Praise God like your life has just begun, with no end.
Respect God's law and precepts, and you will be blessed.

GOD IS ALL THAT IS GOOD

All that is good came from our Creator.
He made heaven a paradise for all believers.
"He created the earth"[28] and embellished it with his beauty.

"He created human beings"[29] and opened the gates of heaven for them to live the real life.
He created the priesthood and gave them immense power in heaven and earth.
"He created heaven"[30], which gives hope to our lives.

He created the angels and saints to magnify and glorify him.
"He created life"[31] so that we can see beauty in us.
"He created heaven" and made it his own sanctuary.

He created the Church and made it a place of joy and love for his faithful to live.
All that he created are greater than good, stronger than strong, lovelier than love.
Purer than pure, mightier than might, and clearer than crystal.

---

[28] Gen 1:1 NJB
[29] Gen 1:27 NJB
[30] Gen 1:1 NJB
[31] Gen 1:25 NJB

YOU'RE FOOLING
YOURSELF, NOT GOD

You're really doing yourself a disservice if you think that you're fooling God by eating at his table and not following his law and precepts. Having faith in God is one thing, but putting his teachings in practice is another.

Tell me.
What good does that do if he feeds you with the finest wheat, quenches your thirst with the finest drink, and you still don't respect one thing in his house?
What sense does that make if you go to church every day and you don't observe his law?

What good does it do if you say all the right things and you don't practice any of them?
Does it make it right for you to be a completely different person outside the Church?
Can you see the big picture and see yourself in "the image of God."?[32]
You think that you are fooling God by saying that you can't relate to his people (the poor).

What is it?
Are you not "created in the image of God" just like them? Are you not a human being just like them?
What good does it do when you tell others what they want to hear, but your mind, body, and soul are empty like a river that runs dry?
What does it do when you tell people what they want to hear and your heart is rotten?

---

[32] Wis 1:23 NJB

Do you really think that God is not watching? He can see you and your actions, wherever you are!

What sense does it make when your speech is not purely from your heart?
Remember that everything from God is pure and holy, so I encourage you to do the same.
Stay clean when approaching the table of the Lord; that way you will save yourself and many around you.

THE KINGDOM OF GOD
IS ELEPHANTINE

The kingdom of God is wiser and broader than anything that you can imagine.

God's teachings do not live in box, nor his vision and his virtue of charity.

We can see the broader picture looking at some of God's creations and extension of his hands.

God created the "earth which has an approximated area of 57,308,738 square miles of land."[33] You can see that he did not create the land for just one city or just one population. He created it for everybody.

He created "the waters which are approximated 139,668,500 square miles,"[34] for everyone to drink and enjoy.

If you look at the wonders that he has created with his bare hands, then you and others can spark magic on your own by spreading the Gospel everywhere and in every place on earth.

God's kingdom and goodness are not limited to just one place or one thing, just like your heart mind, strength, and love.

God sees the big picture in everything that he does, everything that he sees, and everything that he touches.

Another example, the Bible: would the Bible come to existence today if there were not culmination of Scriptures by the Septuagint. It would not come to existence if there was not a collective effort.

I wonder if I would be able to get the good news here today, if our Lord Jesus Christ and the apostles had in mind of proclaiming the Gospel in just Bethlehem, Galilee, or only in Tarsus.

---

[33] www.Zo.Utexas.edu.

[34] www.nationsonline.org.

Can we see what would happen? Most people in this world barely read Scriptures and the Bible and listen to the teaching of the Magisterial. In order to fly home with this lesson today, I want you to understand that God's kingdom does not live, teach, and exemplify in one place but throughout the world.

St. Paul the apostle stated himself that, "Charity is the Greatest virtue of all,"[35] so do not limit yourself to what you can do for yourself. Do things for God and others. It's the same way with charity and proclaiming the good news. Always see the big picture, which you can manifest. Profess that in order to strengthen God's kingdom.

---

[35] 1 Cor 13:13 NJB

GOD IS EVERYTHING
THAT YOU NEED

Let God be your light, let him be your Savior.
Let God be the one who gives you that abundant love.
Let his power flow over you to give you strength.

Don't be so intractable; let him lead you to the promised land.
Make some judicious decisions; go to him for guidance.
Let the Lord lead you to a place you've never been before.

God's law is docile, pure, and tranquil, ready to open the eyes of many.
His law is what needs to be in your heart to deracinate your confusion.
God's law is the one that can revitalize your mind and spirit.

God's law is conducive at every angle that you can see and cannot see.
His love transpires many and changes lives of many for good.
God is lenient toward many who have sinned against him. He is a God who is always ready to forgive.

Holiness is what you need to strive for in this life, in order to be ready for the next life.
God's presence will induce a lively spirit into your life.
Let your heart firmly acquiesce to his law so that you can unify yourself with him one day in heaven.

PUT YOURSELF IN GOD

Put your "mind, heart, body, and soul"[36] into God's hands, and you will not fail.
Focus on him like a laser beam, and you will not be disappointed.
Let God be the vehicle of your soul that can lead you to the promised land.

Put your hard work into God's missions; it will not go in vain.
See yourself as a child of God, and you will be remembered.
Clothe yourself with everything that is good and pure, and you will be honored.

Serve your Master with your full heart, and the gate of heaven will be opened wide for you.
Preach only the good things, and your Father will smile.
Be sincere, genuine, forthright, and others will not be disappointed in you.

Always set the bar high so that others can see the grace and the perfection of our Lord within you.

---

[36] Lk 10:27 NJB

WITH YOU I AM SAFE

O God of gods, Lord of lords!
Under your wings I put my trust, and under your shadow I will find safety.
The devil tries to excoriate me and eat me alive but cannot get near me because your
armies are protecting me.

Your armies are standing by me, from north to south and from east to west.
The devil cannot get near because you are with me all day long and your protection is impervious to violation and unclean minds and spirits.

Your might stretches out throughout, from one end of the universe to the other, and everyone knows that your power is immense.
With you there are no worries because you are true to your words and straight to the point.
Lord, under you wings I'll rest my mind, body, and soul, and safety will be mine.

IT'S TIME

Your time is near, and so is your world.
It's time to repent, time to put all the craziness behind.
It's time to leave all of the vanities and all ungodly things behind.

You still have time to repent all your sins, time to ask the Creator for forgiveness.
It's time to have a deep contrition for you sin and reconcile with others that have been hurt by you.
It's time to cleanse yourself from all of the unclean objects and spirits.

It's time to say, "God, I am all yours. Forgive me, Lord, for all the chaos that I have caused for all the people that I have hurt, and for all the sins that I have committed."
It's time to say, "Lord, take me; here I am."
He will forgive you. He is a God of mercy, and he knows that you're weak.

He's a God of love, and he knows that you are gullible. He is a God of truth, and he knows that you have deceived others in the past, but he is ready, ready with his arms open to take you back
because he is your God, and he is the only God who can save you.

WHAT A MARVELOUS GOD

O God of mercy, God of hope, God of love, God of life,
Everything that is good is you.
Everything that was created by your hands is alive and pure.

"You have created human beings out of nothing and made them in your own image."[37]
You opened the gates of heaven to all of those who follow your law and your precepts.
You've sent us a King that the world cannot contain, a King to rule over the universe.

What a destiny. He was a King before he entered his Mother's womb. What a testimony!
A King that the world had no patience to see, "born in the image and the likeness of man."
He has transformed a world that was about to crash into ashes.

Born to be the leader of the universe with his unlimited capacities and capabilities.
Born to lead his children to the beatific vision, where the love is overflowing.
Born to be the greatest leader to ever touch his foot on earth.

---

[37] Gen 1:27 NJB; Gen 2:7 NJB

GOD CREATED IT ALL

God is great! How great is he?
He created angels that cry out for our forgiveness.
"He created a sun"[38] that shines all over the earth.
"He created a moon that lights over the world."[39]

God created a Church that nourishes his people with all the goods
on a quotidian basis.
He created his priests to administer his forgiveness.
He created the Eucharistic bread and wine to feed his people and to
enter into his life, death, and resurrection.

God created a law that is above and beyond every other law.
He allowed us to come to its perfection.
"He created heaven"[40] and allows us to enter it.

What a world that is! A world of God where everything is at its
perfection.

---

[38] Gen 1:16 NJB
[39] Gen 1:4 NJB
[40] Gen 1:1 NJB

CONFORM YOURSELF TO GOD

When you give to charity, is it not a waste; it ameliorates the life of others.

When you show love to others, it's not in vain because you are cleansing your soul.

When you see others as yourself in a good way, the world is at rest.

When you do not discriminate, the world is at peace.

When you do keep all the knowledge for yourself, pride is not obsolete.

When you see God in every human being, you are at a different level.

When "the image of God"[41] is the same as yours, then God lives in you.

When you don't subterfuge your neighbors, then you are perfecting God's law.

When everything that you do is in God's presence, then the world can breathe.

When everything that you do carries "the image of God,"[42] then your work is not in vain.

---

[41] Wis 1:23 NJB
[42] Gen 1:26-27 NJB

WITH YOUR HELP, THEY CAN FOLLOW YOUR PATH

Lord, your kingdom is at hand. The world is in the midst of a crisis. The lives of your children are being destroyed continually on quotidian basis.

Your children are at risk and confused with all the baggage that the master of all deceits is throwing at them.

Where can they go? Where can they find their Savior? Where can they find their Lord?

Help your children to get out of these quandaries, help them to see the light, help them to be bound by your words, your law, and to revitalize your spirits.

You are the fountain of hope, love, life, caring, and the safety net for all your children.

Help those who are vulnerable to the beast.

Help them to stay strong in their commitment to your law, to stay humble and steadfast against the beast.

Help them to not be so gullible to the lies of the beast.

Help them to rescind all the communication with the beast.

Help them, Lord, to be the children that you have created.

HELP US TO BE GOOD CITIZENS

Lord, you are the light that I see when there is no darkness.
You are the love that makes my world chant.
You are the King that I can count on when I am under duress.
Lord, you are incomparable, immutable, irreplaceable: evidence of your living presence can be seen in the hearts of all the faithful.

With you there is life inside our hearts, light inside our minds, and hopes in our willingness.
Help us be obedient and loyal to you, Lord. You feed us with all the goods every single day.
Help us to respect everything that is attributed to your law, to see the protection and the care that you are continually giving us.
Help us to stop living in this fantasy world and do what is respectable and acceptable to you.

God, help us to come to grips that with you our world is brand-new, safe, calm, and at peace.

HELP US TO FIX OUR MINDS IN YOU

Always stay focused and be diligent about what you see, what you do, and what you say because the devil has misanthropic visions and a deceitful brain.

Watch your lips, your thinking, and your actions because the devil tries to vitiate you, corrupt your mind, and deprave your beautiful heart.

The devil has nothing good but a corrupt mind, a heart full of lies and hebetude.

The devil is extremely blatant and congruous when it comes to love because love does not exist in the devil.

The devil is also capricious. The devil will tell you all the good things so that he can trap you, and then you are on your own.

So don't listen to anything that the devil has to tell you, because he is the master of all deceits.

The devil will show you his artificial paradise, but it's an earthly paradise, and it leads you to nowhere that is good: it's nothing but a one-way ticket that leads you to fierce fire.

YOUR MIGHT

O, God of the universe, let the world see your might so that they may know you are their God and their King.

O, God of the mountains, let them know that your kingdom and creations are firm like a rock.

O, God of the seas, you have commanded the seas to do as you please; command the earth do your will.

O, God of the rivers, you command the rivers to flow in a pattern that is cohesive to your love.

Command hearts to beat in the pattern of your love.

O, God of love, let them see that your love is wrapped up in the mystery of Trinity and divinity.

O, God of peace, let the "river of peace flow"[43] through the hearts of the world that are in turmoil.

Let the world see that your heart is in those that carry your image.

Let the evildoers know that their time is only transitory.

O, God, calm the world's ocean, which is at rage and needs your help to be at peace.

---

[43] Isa 66:12 NJB

YOU ARE CREATED BY GOD TO DO GOOD, NOT EVIL

You are not here to do evil, even though evil is in your blood.
You are not here to hate, even though hate is in mind.
You are not here to judge others, even though that's what the devil wants you to do.

You are not here to be a spectator instead of doing what is good for society.
You are not here to excoriate or subterfuge your brothers and sisters with your lips.
You are not here to imitate the master of all deceit.

You are here to love Christ, and Christ only, with "your whole heart, mind, and soul."[44]
You are not here to be a fainéant but to do the work that will prepare for the beatific vision.
You are not here for greed that will lead you to avarice, lust, and pride.

---

[44] Lk 10:27 NJB

CHRIST'S MIRACLES CAN
WORK ON YOU AS WELL

"Open the eyes of the blind"[45] one more time.
Soften the heart of stoic ones.
Emancipate the minds of those who live in the bubbles.

"Make the cripple man walk again"[46] for the sake of the living.
Open the ears of the dead so that they can hear the good news.
Open your wings and let them see your mighty power.

Open your mouth and let your children hear your beautiful voice.
Choose your army to guard your children's tents and your band to
play your symphony.
Open the gates of heaven for all of those who follow you and believe
in you.

---

[45] Isa 42:7 NIV
[46] Mt 9:2 NIV

HE IS TRUE

The Word of God is true and full of beauty, so as his noble army,
his company, and his law.
The love of God is real, so as his kingdom.
The army of God is strong, so as his power.

The angels of the Lord stand by him, so as his saints and his children,
to pay their dues to the King of glory.
The children of God sing to him to give him praise.

The priests and the clergies of God preach his Gospel and promulgate
his law, a law that is here to stay.

LET OTHERS SEE GOD IN YOU

Congratulations on your success. God loves successful people.

You think that you are above everyone else, just because you drive a fast car and have a nice house.

You have a family whom you treat well; therefore you have some good in you. Don't leave your glass half-empty; fill it up with the presence and spirit of God.

You think that your feet can't touch the ground because of your delusion to think that your world is better than everyone else's.

You think that your success is sufficient enough to be prejudiced and to discriminate against others.

You think that your earthly label gives you the right to vilify, disrespect, and even disregard the law of God.

It's a good thing to be successful, but can't you see that you are missing the train?

Respect others as you respect yourself, love others as yourself, and think of others as yourself.

If you can't relate to those that you are serving, then you are in the wrong field. You are barking up the wrong tree.

If you can't see God in the one that you serve, then you are doing yourself a disservice, you are alienating yourself from God and the people that you are supposed to service.

Wake up, my brothers and sisters! See God in every human being and everything that makes you think of God.

Stay away from all the things that are useless, all the vanities, all the things that can keep you out of God's reach, anything that can sour the heart of the Holy Spirit. Be the one who loves and who shows love to others. Be the disciple of God.

Unify your success with the Trinity and divinity. Don't put all your eggs in one basket; diversify, balance your life with the faith and the law that God is giving to you.

That way, you will save yourself and all the others who look for guidance and the presence of our Lord Jesus Christ to seal your fingerprint in the service of God, make your Father proud. Be that catalyst. Unify your good spirit with the Spirit of God.

IT'S TIME FOR US TO ACKNOWLEDGE THE TRUTH AND TO LIVE IN GOD'S PRESENCE

Born as sinners, life as sinners, and death as sinners.

There is nothing good in us if attributes, our work, our minds, and ourselves are with the devil.

There is nothing good in us if we saturate ourselves in the work of the devil.

The love of God cannot prosper in our presence if we do not see God in us and in every single human being that we come in contact with.

Our hearts cannot beat at the right pace in the rhythm of love that God himself gave us.

If it were for some of us, there would not be a seventh day for God to rest: he would be restless.

There would not be a twelve-hour day but all darkness.

If it were for some of us, life would not have a name, a meaning, or purpose and would not continue: death would be the norm for all eternity.

But with God, everything that is dead comes to life, everything obscure becomes to crystal clear, and everything that is dark comes to light.

It is time for us to come to the acknowledgment that we are nothing without God and we are everything in his existence.

KEEP HIS FLAME BURNING

Gather the family. The feast is about to begin. Give praise to the one we love and the one who loves us.

Show our love for the King of glory with everlasting love, the Lord of lords and God of gods.

Show your brothers and sisters, your neighbors that he is the living presence in your heart and in your life.

Show your fellow human beings that his love is true and spreads throughout the entire world.

Show that he is the God of mercy and forgiveness.

Tell your brothers and sisters that there is no other God like him.

"Keep his flame of love burning in your heart, mind, and soul."[47]

Help illuminate a world that is in darkness.

Help share his love that we are carrying in our hearts.

Help save a world that is capsizing and help bring the children our God.

---

[47] Lk 10:27 NJB

THERE IS NO OTHER LIKE YOU

O Almighty, there can be no other God like you.
"You have created the world,"[48] and you embellish it with your own beauty.
"You have created human beings to curry your own image."

"You have created the sun, the moon, the stars," and they are bright like you.
"You have created the rivers," and they sing your name while flowing and giving life to the needy.
"All of the creatures sing and praise your name."[49]

"You have created the heaven," where the pure rest, and "the earth," where the impure unrest.
O Lord, you can never be obsolete but ever present.
The sea can be enraged, thunder can be roaring, the earth can be shaking; nothing can change you.
You are God forever, and your power can never be decreased but increased.

---

[48] Gen 1:1-31 NJB
[49] Ps 145:21 NJB

STAY TRUE TO HIS MESSAGE

Stay positive. Keep the attitude of God's presence in your heart because that will change the world.

His presence in your heart can make it rain where there is dry land. His love is ever present and infinite. His love can have a greater positive impact on your life and on the lives of others.

His might and power can give strength to your weaknesses and by dying on the cross for you can make you see that his love is real and has no limit for you.

By sharing his bread and wine, his blood and his body, you can help come to understand that his love for you all is beyond compare.

By giving his life to save the world, he showed you that he is a God of love. It should also help you to realize and recognize that "there is no other God like him."[50]

---

[50] Isa 45:5 NJB

SAVE A POOR SOUL

O Lord, renew my existence into your living presence.
Save a poor heart that is on the brink of crashing.
Save a poor soul that is in peril and nothing can save it but you.

Save a poor mind that is sporadic.
Save a poor vision that has nowhere to go but in the dungeon.
O Lord, carry a poor body that is jaded, full of weaknesses, and make
it your own.

OBEY GOD

Obey your superior just like the disciples obeyed our Lord Jesus Christ.
Obey your priests and clergy who administer God's forgiveness.
Obey your local authority, your bishops, because they are the successors
of the apostles.

Obey the doctrine that keeps God new and alive.
Obey the Gospel that is sure, pure, infallible, immutable, and comes
at no cost to you.
Obey the law that is here to stay and to purify your soul.

Obey your God for his love has no limit and is never ending.
Obey the deposited faith that has been given to you by God with the
help of the pope, the bishops, and diocesans.
Obey all that is God and all that is attributed to God.

CHOOSE YOUR ROUTE

God wants everyone to be saved and to be in his company.
It's up to each individual to follow the right path that leads to God.
Also, remember that you are en route to heaven, and hell starts right here on earth.

God gives you free will out of love, but do not abuse it; do not put yourself in a situation where there is no turning back.
Do not separate yourself from God's law and his teachings.
Always remember to do good, and only good, no matter what you encounter.

Again, your ticket to heaven or hell starts here on the earth and ends one step after you enter the gates of heaven, or the bottom pit, based on what you have accomplished and what you have to offer God.
Remember to follow the "Ten Commandments,"[51] Follow God's law and his precepts. Do philanthropic work throughout the world.

Make yourself available to God in every aspect of your life so that you can save yourself and be like God.

---

[51] Ex 20 NJB; Deut 5 NJB

CHRIST'S LOVE

Christ's love and his kindness are brighter than the stars in the sky. His wisdom is brighter than the sun, smoother than oil, and brighter than our intelligence.
His care is tender like his Father, his Mother, and his love carries us through, even when the obstacles seem to have the upper hand.

Christ's might is mightier than the universe and more powerful than anything that we can imagine.
His heart beats in the rhythm of life and his love, which spreads throughout the entire world.
His faithful ones will praise him and love him forever for his love for us never fails.

Christ's visions are so fresh, they are like "Pishon, Gihon, Tigris and Euphrates that flows in the Garden of Eden."[52]
His Spirits are life, love, and hope that bring us into his life.
His clergies, prophets, all his lay people and his assembly will bless him and love him forever because he is nothing else but true and divine.

---

[52] Gen 2:10–14 NIV

IN THE GARDEN

"In the garden of Gethsemane"[53] where his love is surely real.
"In the garden of Gethsemane" where love meets suffering and his mother could not rest.
"In the garden of Gethsemane" where death and sorrow save the human race.

"In the garden of Gethsemane" where the earth has shaken and the wind has blown with anger.
"In the garden of Gethsemane"where our Savior said to John, "son behold your mother and the mother behold your son."[54]
"In the garden of Gethsemane" where darkness ruled, only to bring good out of evil.

"In the garden of Gethsemane" where the Son cried out for the love of his people.
"In the garden of Gethsemane" where love met passion and where the cry of one man helped save the world.
"In the garden of Gethsemane" where his love for us is beyond compare.

"In the garden of Gethsemane" where the Son is obedient to the Father.
"In the garden of Gethsemane" where the new King was crowned and heaven was ready to welcome him.

---

[53] Mt 26:36 NJB
[54] Jn 19:27 KJV

GOD CANNOT BE FOOLED

Are you professing the truth that has been given to you?
Have you passed on his message to his believers and nonbelievers?
Are you fighting for those who are under your care?

Are you crying for peace where you see trouble, violence, and destruction?
Are you crying for justice where there seems to be none?
Have you put yourself in the shoes of those who are suffering?

Do you see yourself in them and God in you?
Do you know what it means to suffer continually?
Don't you have a heart like everyone else, or is it beating at a different pace than others?
Do you see yourself as one race and one kind?

You pretend that you are crying for peace in one place, and you are the master of destruction in another.
Tell me that you cannot change for the good.
Are you comforting those who are in sorrow and feeding those who are dying of anger, like your Father wants you to do?

Can you take a look at yourself in the mirror and tell me that a child of God cannot change his evil ways to be a changed person as a servant of God?
Tell me that you are not part of Christ's redemption.

Are you making every single step and effort to help yourself and others and strengthening God's kingdom, or are you just fooling yourself?
Just remember!

God sees your every move and every step that you make. "Don't delude yourself: God is not to be fooled; whatever someone sows, that is what he will reap."[55]

God cannot be fooled by any unworthy creature, nor can he be fooled by his own company.

---

[55] Gal 6:7 NJB

IF YOU LOVE HIM

If you love him, you can carry the cross for him like Simon did.
If you "love your neighbors,"[56] you can carry the cross for them too.
If you want peace in the world, you can help rescind injustice and prejudice and also help nullify erroneous teachings in order to strength his kingdom.

If you love him, you can follow his lead, his law, and his precepts.
If you love him, you can love everything that is attributed to him.
If you love him, you can love yourself and others unconditionally.

If you love him, you can bring a new face into the world today.
If you love him, you will never cease to seek after him.
If you love him, "yourself and your neighbors,"[57] heaven is the limit.

[56] Mk 12:30 NIV
[57] Mk 12:30 NIV

REST IN PEACE

"Rest in peace"[58] for your death is a new beginning, not the end.
"Do not weep"[59], because your death is the genesis of a new life in you.
"Rest in peace" for he's a judge of mercy, and he will show compassion.

"Rest in peace" because death has no power over your soul.
"Do not weep" because his angels are ready to sing with you.
"Rest in peace" for your God is ready to meet you in his sanctuary.

"Rest in peace" because there is life after death, where you will see the fullness of his love.
"Do not weep" because life in heaven is better than "frankincense, myrrh and gold."[60]
"Rest in peace" because your death will bring smiles into heaven and his noble army is ready to embrace you with open arms.

---

[58] Isa 57:2 NIV
[59] Neh 8:9 NIV
[60] Mt 2:11 NIV

THEY WANT TO DESTROY ME

O God, they are threatening to destroy your kingdom.
Your foes are creating chaos and turmoil in every part of the world..
When will you respond to this madness that is going on?
When will you show them that there is one ruler in the universe and
it is you?

When will you show them that their trouble is only transitory?
When will you destroy the enemy of the whole human race?
When will the world be at peace for the sake of your children?

When will you show them that you are the God of all?
When will they know that the world is in the palm of your hands?
When will the violators stop their malicious intent?

When will they surrender to your law?
When will their evildoings come to crash?
When will you show them that there is no other God but you?

GOD OF ALL

God of Bethlehem, show them your mighty power.
God of Galilee, show them that you are in charge.
God of the sea, show them that you have the power to rule the universe.

God of the rivers, show them your stronghold.
God of hosts, show them your power is undeniable.
God of the earth, show them your immense power.

God of heaven, show them that your power is real and the only true one.
God of heaven, let them know that there is no sanctuary better than yours.
God of the universe, let them be your foot stools. Make them bow down to your law and your precepts because you rule the world with your great power and might.

ALL CREATURES

"All the creatures"[61] of the sea sing for the Lord.
"All the creatures" of the earth sing for you and praise your name.
"All the flying birds"[62] sing your name and praise you.

All of the finest bands praise you and play music in your name because your love never fails.
All of the cantors, the sopranos, the basses, and the altos sing and praise your name.
All the lay people sing and praise your name continually.

All of your children sing and praise you because you gave us life and we need your praises.

---

[61] Gen 1:21 NJB
[62] Rev 19:17 NIV

EVERYTHING HE TOUCHES

Abnormality is not his way; everything that he made is perfectly created.
Everything that he touches becomes clean and pure.
Everything that he sees, he changes it into goodness.

Everything that he embraces is full of love and perfectly harmonious.
Everything that is good is in his courtyards.
Everything that he does goes according to his plan.

Everything that he touches turns into gold and diamond.

THEY WANT NOTHING
BUT DEATH FOR ME

They have prepared a furnace for me, to turn me into ashes. What they don't know is that they prepared their own death.

The furnace is bigger and hotter than any furnace that I have ever seen. They prepared to end my life but fell into the furnace themselves; they don't know that my Lord is with me everywhere I go and every place that I have stayed.

They have prepared to strike me without cause because in them there is no life but death.

In them there is no truth but lies, and in them there is no purity but abnormality.

In them there is no light but darkness. There is no active player but pretender.

In them a heart that beats is obsolete, and a love that cures is never found. They have tried and tried to annihilate me, but their plan has come to nothing.

They have tried to destroy everything that carries my name, but my Lord is with me. My God is a God of safety and love. He has hidden me "under the shadow of his wings,"[63] and no evil can come close to me.

My Lord has hidden me in his sanctuary, where there is no violation, only love.

I will keep my faith in him because I know that I have been loved by God and in his hand safety is the norm.

---

[63] Ps 63:7 NJB

STAY ON GUARD

Listen to God and make yourself available to him because the devil has nothing good to offer.

Everything that the devil offers to you is a trap, and every method that the devil has used and uses is fallacious.

Keep your eyes fixed on God. Be the child that he wants you to be; be the servant that he wants you to be.

Keep your eyes on God. Be that steward, that paragon that he wants you to be for everyone around you.

Stay focused on God. Don't get distracted by the devil and be negligent because you have a ladder to climb. You must stay on track, and you should start now before it's too late.

You should keep God's commandments and his precepts.

You should keep his image inside of you and around you because in him everything is true and vibrant.

SEARCH FOR THE TRUTH

Live in God because God lives in you.
Love God, yourself, and your fellow citizens because God's love is your image.
Search for God, and you will find him because he is your safety net.

Search for God, and you will find love.
Search for life, and God will give it to you.
Search for the truth, and you will find it in your heart.

Think of God, and your mind and your life will be brighter.
Be transformed in your speeches, conduct. See yourself in God, and you will change many hearts for the goodness of God.
Stay true to his law, and he will show you heaven.

CARRY THE TRUTH

Always do your Father's work. You will never get lethargic, and you will always be full of energy.

Be a servant of God because he is a God of love, hope, and pity, and he is always faithful to his children.

Give your heart to God, and he will show you the way and clothe you with the finest clothes.

Always carry the truth with you. You will get the trust of many, and God will protect you.

Always speak the truth with the tongue that he gives you and help make the world better.

Walk in the presence of God, and you will never be alone, and you will be blessed.

THE DEVIL IS AFTER ME

While in trouble, I looked for help. My Lord heard me and answered me.
While I was on the verge of being thrown off the cliff, my Lord grabbed me by my hand and saved me.
My enemies wanted me to be buried alive, but my Lord was with me.

They have tried everything that they can do to destroy me, my life, and my soul, but there is no progress in this malicious intent because my Lord is at my side.
They have their arrows pointed at me, but nothing can reach me because my God is with me and he hides me in his tabernacle.
They were dumped under the deep blue sea, but I swam like a fish and came out untouched.

They want nothing but death for me, but my God will protect me as long as I live.

PUT EVERYTHING IN GOD

When darkness comes to you, put yourself in God.
When the world is against you, put yourself in God.
When your world is on the verge of crashing, put yourself in God.

When your world is in the verge of drowning, put yourself in God.
When your world is in deep trouble, put yourself in God.
When your good ideas are not going according to plan, put yourself in God.

When trouble finds you, put yourself in God.
When darkness follows you, put yourself in God.
When your God is the only answer, put yourself in him.

COME TO HIM

Come and bathe in the water that is clean and pure.
Come and bathe in the water that regenerates your life and your soul.
Come and bathe in the water that rescinds your sins and brings you to life.

Come and bathe in the water that opens the eyes of many.
Come and bathe in the water that is always fresh and perfect.
Come and revitalize yourself in the fountain of life.

Come bathe yourself with an everlasting love.
Come and calm your world in the presence of God.
Come and get anointed with the oil of God.

Come and immerse yourself in the Spirit of God.
Come and feel the love that the Holy Father has for you.
Come and let your life be a temple of the Holy Spirit.

YOUR LIFE IN GOD

Your life in God is secure and at peace.
Your life in God is being renewed every single day.
Your life in God brings your life to another level.

Your life in God brings smiles into the face of the earth.
Your life in God shows the path to holiness.
Your life in God brings joy to the ears and hearts.

Your life in God brings union into the world.
Your life in God makes heaven smile.
Your life in God shows his love for humanity.

HOLINESS

Holiness is a way of a true life, and it comes from a true divine.
Holiness is the greatest gift in the game and the path to life.
Holiness is the way to heaven and the greatest accomplishment, which is wrapped up in the mystery of God.

Holiness is God's way of telling us that everyone has a chance.

Holiness is the way of perfection when it comes to God.
Holiness is God's love that is manifested in "our heart, soul, strength, and mind."[64]
Holiness is nothing less than the beatific vision.

---

[64] Lk 10:27 NJB

MAKE GOD PRESENT IN YOUR LIFE

Watch those who carry his image with them and see how they live their lives.

Use their examples as your own and their image as your own because it's been passed to them from God, and the journey needs to be continued so that prosperity can be flourished.

Use the examples of God to enlighten those who don't have a clue about who God is and bring clarity to their confusions.

Live your life in the image of God, show the world the true life that your Father has created in you, and share the love that God has established in your heart and soul.

Bring heaven to their thinking and clean their hearts with the purest water.

WHATEVER YOU WANT
WILL COME TO YOU

If you want peace, it will follow you wherever you go.
If you want love, it will come to you in a timely manner.
If you want life, it will be yours.

If you are not avaricious and thrifty, you will continue to give and
you will receive.
If you "love God and your neighbors,"[65] your name will be written in
the book of holiness.
If you want to strive, you will survive with the strength of your God.

If your heart is clean and pure, you will be in his tabernacle.
If you love God and everything good around you, he will be with you.
If you are searching for the truth, God is the answer for that truth.

---

[65] Lk 10:27 NJB

THEY SAID

They said, "Wisdom came from God," but you have to search for it.
They said, "Love came from God," but you have to strive for it.
They said, "Being faithful is a great thing," but you have to allow it
to flow in your spirit.

They said, "Loving God is beautiful," but you also have to love yourself
as well as your neighbor.
They said, "Knowledge came from God," but you have to search for
it, and it only comes to you when you are ready to take it to the next
level.

They said, "God is good," but you have to live in his presence.
They said, "God is grace," but it can only come to you when you
follow his law.
They said, "God is love," but you can only see it every day if you look
for it in his goodness and his Spirit.

HE ONLY CARES ABOUT YOUR GOODNESS

God does not care about how much money you have in the bank. He does not care about how many portfolios you have diversified.

He does not care about the size of your house or the kind of vehicle that you drive.

He cares about your well-being, and he wants you to come to him.

God does not care how much land you have on this earth.

All that he cares about is that you have a clean heart and soul and a pure mind that will lead you to him.

He does not care about how many stocks you have in the stock market; all he cares is that you follow the law that is written in your heart.

All God cares about is that you live your life as his child and treat everyone with dignity and respect so that you can live in his presence.

FOLLOW GOD

Follow God, and he will take the devil's seed out of your heart.
Follow God, and he will not let you down one bit.
Follow God, and he will be a safety net for you.

Follow God, and you will be invisible to your enemies.
Follow God, and nothing unclean can touch you.
Follow God, and you will be "under the shadow of his wings."[66]

Follow God, and he will protect you from all that is impure and unclean.
Follow God, and he will be "the stronghold for your safety."[67]
Follow God, and you will be loved for eternity.

---

[66] Ps 17:8 NJB
[67] 2 Sam 22:3 NJB

DON'T LET THE DEVIL
TAKE OVER YOU

Do not let the devil get in the way of what leads you to God.
Do not let the devil take over your life.
Say all good things to people around you; always stay positive.
Show that you care for them and love them like your Father.

Do not let the devil make your decisions for you.
All the decisions that you are making and planning on making, always
make sure that they are in accord with your Lord, your God.

Do not let the devil manipulate you because the devil is the master
of all deceit and the enemy of the whole human race.
Do everything according to God's law and precepts.
Stay away from anything that stands in opposition of God.

Stay close to God and embrace everything that is attributed to God.
Pave your future and follow the path to holiness.

GOD OF ALL

O God of North and South America, you come before everything, and everything good comes to existence after you.

O God of Europe, you've created the world and rule it by your own might.

God of Africa, everything that you have created has its own natural beauty.

O God of Asia, you have created everything with your own hands, and from that we can see nothing but the testimony of a true living God.

O God of Australia, you have created the seas and the rivers, and they all give you praise.

God of Antarctica, everything good belongs to you and your company.

O God of the universe, you have created human beings and let make the wonder of your hand.

There is no other God like you. In your presence, everything is calm and alive.

O God of all, you have created oxygen and make it the source of life for all the living creatures.

O God of light, you have created heaven, and only those with pure and clean hearts can get there.

O God of love, you have created the plants and the flowers, where your beauty is manifested for all to see.

THEY ARE TRYING TO DESTROY ME

I wake up in the morning, and a legion is after me to destroy my life, but my Lord is with me.

At midday, they come after me, trying to obliterate me; they want nothing but death for me.

I am not afraid because my Lord is with me. I am not afraid because with God my life is impervious to the violators.

At night, the army of many divisions and brigades try to come after me, but not a hair will come out of my skin because I am a child of God, and he "keeps me under the shadow of his wings.

Under the shadow of his wings is where I rest."[68] Under his tent is where my life is, and I am not afraid because God is with me day and night.

---

[68] Ps 63:7 NJB

IMPERVIOUS TO THEIR WRONGDOING

They are searching for me to harm me, but they can't see me, and I am right next to them.

They cannot touch me because their hands are unclean and their minds are corrupted.

They have tried to infiltrate all of their agendas into those who are gullible and have poor souls.

They want to destroy everything in me; there is nothing good in them but venom and poison.

Day and night they go after me, but they will know that my heart and soul are in God's hands.

I am not afraid because my Lord is at my side at all times.

Every step that I make, God is right there by my side, and every route that I take, he is next to me to project me from the wolves because he is a God of love, and he will never leave me as long as I am faithful to his law.

HE IS WITH YOU

Wherever you see love, there is also life.

Whenever you meet God, there is also love.

Wherever you see hate, there is nothing but death, destruction, and Satan.

Whenever you give a hand to the needy, God's work is at perfection.

Whenever you put his love to use, you are not alone, and God is with you.

Whenever you give your life to him, it's not in vain. He will be waiting for you in heaven.

Whenever you see his people, you will know them by their names and by their actions.

Wherever there is a real smile, there is also a real love.

Wherever you carry his love, he is there with you.

DO WHAT IS ACCEPTABLE TO GOD

Can we have the same positive law for the poor and the rich?
Can we treat everyone with dignity and respect?
Human law is prejudiced, unclean, impure, and rotten; there is merely nothing good in it.
God's law is what we need. It does not discriminate. It's clean, pure, true, broad-minded, and full of greatness and love.

Can the law and the love of God flow through our systems so that we can be impervious to the seed that the devil wants to plant in us? We live in a world today where some of those who are supposed to protect the positive law and the natural law have no respect for any of them.
How can one respect God's law if he does not respect his own?
Can we have a conversation about how to respect human lives?

Can we respect the lives that God has created on this earth?
Can we understand that our lives depend on theirs and their lives depend on ours?
Can we bring peace to our conversation and not always end in the argument about who is right or wrong?
When it comes to human lives, you have no right to destroy any because you are not the Creator! God is!

God has created you to do good and only good.
God has also created you to fulfill his law, so respect your life and all of the other lives around you so that you can be saved by God.

BY THE ACTION YOU WILL KNOW
THE GOOD AND THE BAD

Satan appeared in the image of Jesus, standing on the street where I live, trying to come into my house with his mean, ferocious beast look, like a five-hundred-pound black bear.

Satan and his company were ready to storm the house so that they could come and eat me alive, but my Lord was with me. My Lord sent two members of his army to protect me. There were two members of God's army sent in the image of two dogs, each about 120 pounds. One was black, and the other was tan. The black one stood on my right hand side, and the tan one on my left side, ready to protect me at any cost.

But Satan and his company disappeared after three seconds when my protectors came to protect me.

Brothers and sisters, pray to the Lord and praise him because when he is with you, he will not leave your side one bit. All you have to do is to be faithful to him and his law.

In the blink of an eye, or one heartbeat, I can see your intention. I can tell that you are the deceitful one, and I can tell that you are not my Savior, Jesus.

When your heart is in God, no devil can fool you. When your mind is fixed on God, nothing can come near your tent.

My Lord is with me day and night, and he will never let any unclean spirits violate me.

Satan! You can try to look like Jesus, but you cannot fool his children. God's children know their God, their Lord, Jesus Christ.

You cannot fool the faithful with your nakedness and your unclean heart and spirits.

You are troublesome, while my Lord is a Mediator.

You are always at war, while my God is at peace.

You always aim at destruction, while my God is always constructing and building.

You are a waste, while my God is truly conducive.

NO UNDERSTANDING

Living in a world of madness where the cows do not recognize the donkeys?

The cat does not recognize the dog, and they go about their business doing their own things.

The birds do not recognize their prey, where the world is speeding is in reverse mode.

The creatures do not recognize their Creator while the world is hanging on a thin thread of a needle.

The violators do not recognize their wrongdoing while they are thinking what's wrong is right.

Where some of God's faithful have failed to recognize his mission and his plans.

Living in a world today where respect is not prevalent while dishonesty and integrity are in question.

Those who are in charge can't seem to understand that violating God's law is unacceptable and abominable.

Keep Satan out of your body and your world and your soul. Follow the true God.

Keep your eyes open at all times; know your prey and your enemy.

Stay strong in prayer and recognize your God and his mission for the world.

THEY DON'T KNOW THEIR REAL GOD

Father! Your children are being enslaved by the devil. They have almost nothing good left in them.
Let freedom ring through "the heart, mind, Strength, and soul."[69]
Their hearts show nothing but emptiness. Lord, fill their hearts with your goodness.

Their hearts have no embracement for love to pass on to others.
Let your abundant love ring inside their hearts. Kiss their hearts with your touch of love and transform them into holiness.
Their memories are ephemeral, which can disappear within the blink of an eye: they don't remember a thing that you did for them.

They live with the devil, they bathe with the devil, they eat with the devil: everything that they do is the opposite to their true and real God.
Father! Please enlighten them and let them see the power of your hand and the goodness of your law.
Let them know that you are the light, the sun, the moon, the stars, the seas, the living bread, love,
and the wisdom that frees them with everything that is good and everything that is bright.

Father! Clothe them with your clothes, "feed them with your finest food,"[70] mold them into you and your law so that they can live in "the image and the likeness of you."[71]

---

[69] Lk 10:27 NJB
[70] Ps 81:16 NIV
[71] Gen 1:26 NJB

THINKING ABOUT YOUR
GOODNESS AND GREATNESS

Staring at the world, thinking of you and thinking about how great you are and how great your provision is.

Thinking about your wonders, and mouth is dwelling and extremely taciturn.

Thinking about your love for the world, and I cannot explain.

Thinking about your doctrine is where my love is.

Thing about your heaven is what I should be focused on.

Thinking about your greatness is what I should be striving for.

Thinking about your holiness is what my mind should be focused on, like a magnet.

Thinking about your goodness is what I should follow in the essence of being like you.

Thinking about your pure and clean heart and what my heart should be like.

Thinking about your inspiration and what I should strive for in order to inspire others.

I AM ALL YOURS

My love still remains in you even when the world is in trouble.
My life is still alive within you, even when I don't think that I can survive.
My future depends on you, Lord, even when I cannot seem to get it right.

My heart remains in you, even when the devil tempts me day and night.
My mind focuses on you, even when I don't have anything good in me.
My world belongs to you, even when I seem to be a perfunctory servant.

My holiness depends on your guidance, even when I can't seem to grasp your law.
My life belongs to you, in everything that I do and everything that I take charge of.
My heart is at your door, and even when I can't seem to love, you are the one who can change me for the good.

You are the one who can metamorphose my love into greatness, and you are the one who has the final word, so please help us to stay true to your word and law.

BE THAT CHILD

You are not supposed to turn your back on your Father.
Your are not supposed to turn your back on the mouth that feeds you.
You are not supposed to abandon his law and his precepts.

You are supposed to be the child of God and to follow him wherever you go.
You are supposed to love God: by loving God you can "love yourself and your neighbor."[72]
You are not supposed to alienate yourself from the one who loves you.

You are supposed to feed yourself with all the good meals that your Father has provided for you.
You are supposed to be inspired by each teaching and inspire others with his words.
You are supposed to have God in you so that you can "magnify Him and praise His name"[73] like a choir praising its king.

---

[72] Mk 12:30 NIV
[73] Lk 1:46 NJB

BRING ME TO LIFE

Lord of all, save a life that is in a quagmire situation and a heart that is shattered in pieces.
Bring to life a lost child and a lost soul.
Make me new like the sunlight in the morning and save a heart that has nothing good to give.

Bring to life the child that is supposed to carry your image.
Make my mind fresh like the water in the Antarctic and the cleanest stream water that has ever existed.
Bring back to life a child of your temple. Make my heart clean like yours and my mind smooth like yours.

Make me brand-new in every corner, at every avenue, and every angle that has existed.
Let me be one more time the wonder of your works and the miracle of your hands.

THEY WANT TO USE ME
AS THEIR MEAL

Lord! They have prepared a table to have me for their dinner. They want me to be their special meal, but I am not afraid because in you I put my trust. Therefore, I will not be their special meal for dinner, nor their dessert, because my Lord is with me, and he will spare me from every danger. God will save me from the mouth of the hyenas. He will save me from the mouth of the wolves.

They wanted to use me as their hunting meal, but I called upon the Lord. He heard me, and he came to my rescue. My God is real. He will not allow me to become anyone's special meal, nor let my soul be violated by the unfaithful. God will not let me down because my faith and my trust have no other place but in him.

God will not let them get near me. What an awesome God! He never loses his temper or my trust.

The roads are treacherous, but with God I am not afraid. I am not afraid because I know that he will protect my soul as long as I am faithful to him.

Now my faith is in the Lord. I will not turn back to the old way. I will be in his heart forever, and no evil can come my way because my mind, heart, and soul belong to God forever.

THEY DON'T REMEMBER
THEIR WRONGDOING

Father, come to their rescue; they can't seem to understand your way. They do not know what is right and wrong; their hearts are incorrigible, and their minds are full of waste.

They are penitent creatures; their wrongdoings bring no fresh air to the atmosphere and no peace to the world.

Evildoing and madness are what they are striving for; nothing is good in them.

They are hostile to everything that they see, everything that they touch, and everything around them.

Your law and their behaviors don't see eye to eye. They are malevolent in every aspect of their lives.

They are intractable to every good advice and wisdom.

Lord! Only you can bring life into these lost souls because no one else can rescue them but you.

THE IMPOSSIBILITY OF LOVING GOD WITHOUT HIS COMPANY

You cannot love God when you detest your neighbors.

You cannot love God when your mind is corrupt, your heart is depraved, and your speech is toxic.

You cannot love God when you don't love yourself.

You cannot give something that you don't have; you cannot provide water from an empty well.

You cannot care for a life that you do not live and do not understand.

You cannot live a life that you do not care for, and you cannot give a gift that you do not have.

You cannot love God if you are irascible, not open, and not willing to take good advice from those who know better than you.

You really don't have it in you, but there is always hope, even when you are steering in the wrong direction.

You can come back to him if you are true and willing to change for the good.

If not, embrace yourself for the fiery lake where there is no turning back, where the heat and ice will rule your world.

I WOULD RATHER BE IN GOD

I would rather not live than to not be in the presence of God.

I would rather climb mountains day and night, with seventy thousand horses on my back than try to find an easy way out and offend my God.

I would rather live poor than not to keep your Spirit in me, a Spirit that gave me life.

I would rather eat grass and live with nothing than to offend your tabernacle.

I would rather live in pain than take the short way and offend your law.

I would rather smile in sorrow than disrespect your house and offend the mouth that feeds me.

I would rather die in hunger than not eat the living bread that you have provided for me to be fed.

I would rather die in vain than to disregard your law and your precepts.

I would rather not be in existence than do the devil's work.

I would rather do good day and night than be in the house of pain and the land of the dead.

I would rather love God, myself, and neighbors than marry the devil and carry hate in my spirit.

I would rather live in God than see the devil eye to eye, and I would rather speak the truth than be like a mule.

YOUR MIND

Your mind is your brother, and your brother is your mind. When one separates itself from the other, that is when you know that you're in a quandary.

Your heart is your love, and your love is your heart. When the two are separated from each other inside your body, that is when you know that you have a paucity of love in you.

Your eyes are your optical views, and what you see is what you are made of and what can enlighten you.

Your love is your life, and your life is what drives you to greatness. If you don't have love in you, there cannot be any life and your world is in trouble.

The truth from your tongue is what can differentiate you from the rest. If you don't have it in you, you are in a different world.

When your brain is disconnected from your body, then trouble lies ahead of you.

When you cannot love your fellow citizens, your world is heading to the devil's house.

Your knowledge is your passport and others' too. If you can't pass it on to others, then it becomes pride, which makes you much closer to the devil than God.

LISTEN TO THE WORDS OF
YOUR FATHER ABOVE!

I am your God and only God! I will save you from the evildoers.
I will spare you from the teeth of the ferocious beasts.
I will save you from getting tramped on by these violators, and I will show them that I am the God of all.

My protection will save you from any attack that they are plotting against you.
I will hide you "under the shadow of my wings."[74] I will let no one get near you because you are a child of mine.
You will keep my law in your heart and my precepts in your soul.
My law is what you will keep as your morning, your midday, and evening.

Be not afraid of anything because I am with you, and I will protect you as long as you keep my law in your "heart, mind, body, and soul,"[75] as long as you give the same love to your brethren and your sister.
I will make you as tall as the sky, as big as the universe, as wise as my spirit, as clean as my temple: you will live in my house forever, and you will become part of me.

---

[74] Ps 17:8 NJB
[75] Lk 10:27 NJB

RESPECT YOUR SPOUSE

Respect the one that God has created you to be with and show her compassion.

Do you respect yourself? If you don't, then you can't respect anybody or anything that is around you.

Don't treat her like a defeated dog. She is your equal, your spouse, your life, and your care.

Respect the covenant that bonded you two together; respect the law that God has established inside of you.

Always say the good things to her. Let her see the presence of the living God in your soul.

Let her taste the living bread that God has created in your heart to feed your hunger and avoid the devil's route.

Avoid carrying out the load and the work that the devil has in store for you.

Never disrespect her, never lay your hands on someone that you love, and never lay your hands on anything that is made by the hand of God.

Love the wife that God has created for you to be with. If she happens to be at fault sometimes, pray for her, and if you happen to be at fault, she will do the same.

It seems to be uncanny to treat someone that you are planning on living your life with in an abominable manner.

If you don't respect your wife, you are a disgrace to society, you are a disgrace to yourself, and you are a disgrace to God.

Respect and love your wife always because that is what you are supposed to do; that is your everyday obligation.

Always take care of the one that you love and always love the one that you care for. If you love someone, you want all the good things for her, and if she happens to be your wife, that is more than an obligation; that is the law in the eyes of God and your fellow citizens.

Let your love for her see the light, and that light will lead you to a better place.

Let your love for her be abundant, like the fall leaves in autumn that are overflowing with love, and God will satisfy your soul.

LET THEM BE

Let your love show how great God is and how great his love is manifested in your heart.

Let the plants be as green as they can be in the garden of God.

Let the earth kiss the sky and let the cloud make rain for the love of God.

Let the rivers flow at their own speed and let the waves of the sea move at their own pace.

Let the air be as clean as it can be and let your heart beat at its own pace.

Let the moon brighten your mind and let the sun shine in your heart.

Let God's love be shared in the manner that it was given.

Let the peacemakers be paragon in your life. Let your spirit be elevated by their love.

Let heaven cry out with joy for the genesis of new life and a new child living in Christ.

WILL NEVER LET ME DOWN

God will never let me down. He will not let me rest in the jungle. God will never let me rest in the hand of the evildoers. God will never let the enemy take me hostage.

God will always be there for me to protect me when I am in trouble. God will shield me in the wake of danger, and I will rest in his courtyard in the light of peace. God will make me firm as a rock when weaknesses try to take over my life.

God will never let me down as long as my faith is in his sanctuary. God will protect me from the impure, the unclean spirits, and he will feed me, like a pelican with a paucity of food still manages to feed its newborns. God will save me when I call upon his name, and under his wings is where I will be.

BY CRYING OUT FOR HELP, SOME SAY

Lord! Are you not listening? Are you not there?
I have called upon your name for help, and there is no answer.
Knocking on your door, but there is not a voice to answer my cry.

I pray and cry out to you for help, and it is as though I do not exist.
When will your child stop suffering and get the help that he needs?
When will you put an end to my misery? When will you wake up a
man that is already dead but still working?

When will you hear your children's cry for your help?
When will you let me see the light at the end of the tunnel, and when
will my life change for the better?
When will my darkness be my daylight, and my sorrow be my joy?

When will you save a child that is so helpless and so desperate for
your help?
When will your child see the land of the living, and when will my
joy be at your rest?

You can ask your Lord, your God, for anything, but just remember to
ask him in a respectful manner!
Just remember the way you ask can impact the way you receive.

I CAN NO LONGER HIDE

When can I see the bright light and the real sunshine?
I cannot wait for the morning and daylight.
I can no longer live in darkness and no longer live in a cage.

I can no longer stay mute but speak your truth.

I can no longer tell lies but live in the truth.
I can no longer hate but love everything that you have created.
My only duty is to see you in every human being, even when they are
not breathing the same air that you are breathing.

I can no longer hide but reveal myself to the world.

I can no longer procrastinate but do the work that you have sent me
to do.
I can no longer retaliate but bear insults.
I can no longer curse but speak with kind words that came from you.

YOU ARE SO GREAT

I will praise you forever because you deserve my praise.
I did not exist, but in you I came to existence.
There was nothing good in me until I saw your light.

My heart was not beating, but you made it sing like a melody.
My life was lost, but you saved it when you baptized me.
My mind was in a different world, but you made it come to life.

I was a tacit child, but you made me so outspoken.
My eyes were closed, but you opened them with your light.
I was among the dead, but you brought me to life.

WHEN YOU SEE HIS PRESENCE

When you see his Spirit in the heart of his people, then you know that he is here.

When you hear great sermons from the priest, then you know that he is here.

When you hear wisdom from others, then you know that he is here.

When you come to the great celebration in his temple, then you know that he is here.

When you see the love of the people around you, then you know that he is here.

When you hear the great speeches containing his name, then you know that he is here.

When you glorify his name, then you know that he is here.

When you feel like you want to be his in his church at all times, then you know that he is here.

When you feel his presence inside of your heart, then you know that he is here.

THE LORD IS YOUR LORD FOREVER

The Lord will be your household forever!
The Lord will save you from all that is harmful to you and your family.
The Lord will never let you be a special meal for the beast and those who do evil.

The blessing of the Lord is in your midst.
The Lord will always be with you in your shining day and rainy night.

The power of God is above all. His might can be seen from one end of the universe to the other.
You will be the Lord's children forever, and you will never violate his law and his precepts.
The Lord will never let any unpleasant creature come between you and him.

HAPPY THE MAN WHO
GIVES HIS LIFE TO GOD

"Happy the man"[76] who does not let vanity take over his life but surrenders to God instead.
"Happy the man" who keeps God's law and precepts in his heart and makes them his own.

"Happy the man" who never gives his soul to the enemy of God!
"Happy the man" who lets God's blessings cherish in his heart and God's love flourish in his actions.

"Happy the man" who takes the kingdom of God seriously and never takes part in the actions of the evildoers.
"Happy the man" who loves nothing but God's people and everything that was created by God.

"Happy the man" who shows love for the poor for the presence of God is in his heart.
"Happy the man" who is the temple of the Holy Spirit for God's grace is upon him.

"Happy the man" who lives in the presence of God for God's kingdom will be his forever.
"Happy the man" who follows God's law and precepts for the kingdom of heaven will be shown to him.

---

[76] Ps 119:2 NIV

HOW COME

You only call God when trouble is at your front door.
You only call God when your mind is on the brink of losing.
You only call God when misery's taking over your shelter.

You only call God when your heart is beating irregularly.
You only call God when your lung is barely pumping air.
You only call God when your mind can't rest.

You only call God when you are not at peace.
You are only call God when your world is upside-down.
You only call God when you need him.

Can you call God day and night? Can you call him regardless of the situation that you are in?
Can you call God and tell him that you love him and there is no other like him?
Can you thank God for the love that he is showing you every day and tell him that his existence is our heartbeat and his care is our oxygen?

You should call God at all times, not just when you need his help!

YOUR GOD

Your God is a God of mercy; you acknowledge him by showing mercy.
Your God is a God of love; you should embrace him.
Your God has everything good to offer; you should love him and follow his lead.

Your God is a God full of trust, and you should trust him with all your heart.
Your God is a God of hope; your faith should be at the same speed as his doctrine.
Your God is a God of truth; you should follow his statutes.

Your God is brighter than daylight and more luminous than nightlight.
Your God has a concrete plan you, and you should follow his plan.
You God will never let you down, as long as you keep his law in your heart and his vision in your mind.

YOU LOVE YOUR GOD

You love your God. Love his people too.
You love his doctrine. Love his priests, nuns, and deacons too.
You love his words. Follow his commandments and his precepts.

You love his way of thinking; think like him.
You love his plan; plan your life around him.
You love his vision; see things the way he sees them.

You love his Spirit; let his Spirit revitalize the spirits of others
through you.
You love his might; embrace his law, and you will be untouchable.
You love him; love his Mother, his people, and his assembly too.

PAY DUE TO YOUR GOD

Pay dues to the living God who loves you unconditionally. Let him see your acknowledgment and your admiration for him.

Pay dues to the Creator of heaven and earth because his hands are wonders.

Pay dues to the God of the universe because he rules the world with his power.

Pay dues to the God of all because there is no other like him.

Pay dues to your Father because he is a Father who loves his children and his love never fails.

Pay dues to the one who never lets you down and is always there with you. All you have to do is be faithful to his law and precepts.

Pay dues to your God, your Lord, because in him life is always new and alive.

Let him be your leader because he is the only true God in the universe and the only one who can save your soul.

Pay dues to the God of love and mercy because he will show you the way and he will always love you.

WHEN GOD IS NEAR

When you hear the Word of God, you will know that he is in your tent. God will never leave you empty-handed. He will have a good provision for you and take good care of you.

When you see the actions of God, you will know that he is near your heart.
God will keep you from all the madness and all the things that are hard to swallow.
He will keep you in his dwelling place at all times.

When you feel the presence of God, you will know that he is in your best interest.
God will be with you forever. He will never let you down.

When you see the love of God, you will know that his love is incomparable.
God's kindness and care are always available to you.

When you see the good deeds of God, you will know that his love and his heart are in you.
God will keep you under his protection, save you from all of those who want nothing but death for you.

When you see that you are impervious to danger, you will know that God is on your side.
God's angels will surround you always, like a shield to protect you from any malicious intent. He is a God who never decreases but increases.

When you see the fullness of God, you will know that his power is mighty, immense, and implacable.

WILL YOU BE READY

Will you be ready when "the trumpets blow?"[77]
Will you be the one coming out of his Church to welcome him?
Will you be the one who did enough in this world to receive his infinite accolades?
Will you be ready when the Son of humankind comes to bring peace to the world?

Will you be ready when you see his face in the sky with great power?
Will you be ready when you see his Mother also appear in the sky, in less than three heartbeats, standing by his upper right side, wearing white and holding the little child on her left arm, folded in a white cloth?
Will you be ready when you see his face only appear in the sky and not his whole body?

Will you be ready when you see his brown ladder suspended in the air with one rope on each side, ready to take you to his sanctuary?
Will you be one of the faithful to climb the ladder of the Lord?
Will you be ready to receive the final word from your Lord, your God?
Will you be one of the faithful with a clean heart that will be with him and praise him forever?

Will you be in his Father's company when "He turns over the Kingdom to His Father?"[78]
Will you be one of his chosen to live the eternal life that was created for all pure minds and clean hearts?

---

[77] Rev 8:6 NJB
[78] 1 Cor 15:24 NIV

CANTICLE OF MIKINSON

Love the Lord.
"All ye"[79] children of the Lord, love the Lord.
"All ye" wing messengers of the Lord, love the Lord.
"All ye" clouds that move in the sky, love the Lord.

"All ye" creatures on earth and heaven[80], love the Lord.
"All ye" faithful of the Lord, love the Lord.
"All ye" Paraclete of the Lord, love the Lord.
"All ye" flowers and blooms, love the Lord for his might has no limit.

"All ye" heroic virtues of the Lord, love the Lord.
"All ye" queens and kings, love the Lord.
"All ye" that keep the precepts of the Lord and his law, love the Lord.

"All ye" luminous objects in the sky, love the Lord.
"All ye" priests, deacons, and faithful of the Lord, love the Lord.
"All ye" mountains and cliffs, love the Lord for his heart is pure and clean.
"All ye" creations of the Lord, love the Lord and praise him for his heart is full of love and ever present.

---

[79] Mt 11:28 KJV
[80] Rev 5:13 NIV

CANTICLE OF MIKINSON

All the angels of the Lord, sing his name.
All the seas, rivers, and stars, give him praise.
All the preachers of the Lord, give him praise.

Paraclete of the Lord, pay his due.
All the lay people of the Lord who love him, spread his love to the world.
Heaven and earth, bless his name and make him proud.

Let his love be in "our minds, bodies, and souls."[81]
"All the creatures of the Lord"[82], praise his name.
All the people of the Lord, follow his lead.

All who are baptized in him, stay on course.
All the children of the Lord, praise his name.
All the ones who love God, love his world.

Let his Spirit be the light of our world.

---

[81] Lk 10:27 NJB
[82] Gen 1:30 NIV

YOUR KNOWLEDGE CAN BE USELESS
IF NOT PAYING ATTENTION

You can be as smart as you can be, the sharpest of all, but if Christ is not in you, you are not among the living.

You can have a brain like a computer and an IQ that no one else has. Your mind can be as sharp as the sharpest sword on earth, but if you don't have Christ in, you are like ravine of waste with a flood running through its core.

You can speak, be fluent in many languages, but if you don't have Christ in you, your heart is rotten and can explode at any time.

You can have the best-paying job in the world, but if you don't have Christ in you, you are like a lost child with a lot of green.

You can be the most acute brain surgeon in the world, but if you don't have Christ in you, your life is lost.

You can be the most popular and the most powerful person on planet Earth, but if you don't have Christ in you, your world is in trouble.

You can have the most beautiful appearance on the outside as a person, but if Christ is not in you, you're just like lipstick on a pig.

You can live in a castle or in the biggest mansion that exists on planet Earth, but if Christ is not in you, there is no life in you.

You can be the poorest of all with your appearance on the outside, but if Christ is in you, you are the richest of all.

If Christ is in you, there is also life in you, which can have a positive impact on others and save humankind.

TAKE GOOD CARE OF THE CHILDREN

The children are the future of the Church, the school, the world. They are the next generation.

Receive them in your heart, just like your God, your Lord, would receive them.

Do you remember what Christ said? "Anyone who welcomes one little child like this in my name welcomes me."[83]

Do not ever abuse or hurt a little child because when you engage in this kind of immorality, you are crushing the heart of our Lord Jesus Christ. You make his heart bleed even more.

When you hurt a little child, you are breaking Christ's heart, the child's heart. You are breaking the future generation's heart.

You will make your Lord suffer more than he did during his crucifixion because a little child is harmless.

You should love them and give them the best treatment that you can ever give to a child.

Think of the child that you see as your own child, your own blood, your own family.

Do not take the route that Satan leads you to hurt a child.

Don't you remember when you were a kid and you wanted toys? You wanted all the good things that ever existed to come your way in order to enjoy life.

You should be the one to give them all the good things that exist, all the great things that they need in order to succeed in life.

You are not here to take their precious innocence away. You are not here to destroy their lives. You are not here to break their spirits. You are not here to inflict wounds inside their hearts.

You are here to treat them well. You are here to share with them the love that your Father has given to you.

---

[83] Mt 18:5 NJB

Remember you were a kid too! They deserve great care and great treatment from you.

Don't ever abuse a child! Never look at him or her in any awkward way. Don't let Satan lead you to destroy their lives.

Don't be the facilitator of Satan! Don't live in the dark side where there might be no return.

Love every child that you see around you because his or her future also depends on you.

Respect the little, precious lives. Give them God's care and protect them whenever or wherever you see any kind of activity that is unjust to them.

You should feel hurt when you see a child being hurt or abused by another.

You should see this child as your own; you should feel that this could have happened to you when you were young.

You should never hurt a child! You should never choose the path of darkness.

You should seek God every time your mind is not working right. You should pray to him to make your path straight. You should love all the children like you love God.

You can't love God without loving his children. It's impossible. You cannot love his Church without loving him, and you cannot love God without loving his community.

You should think twice before you take the path of Satan. You should examine yourself before thinking about hurting or abusing a harmless child.

Just remember the path to heaven or hell starts right where you are, and when you leave this world, your God, your Lord, will make the final decision based on how you treat his children on this earth.

Now you have the power to choose what your future is going to be. You can choose the path for eternal life or the path to the bottom pit.

SUNDAY MORNING 09/19/15, 6:53 A.M.

$\mathcal{I}$ was at a mass at St. Mary's Church in Crown Point, Indiana, and Rev. Patrick J. Kalich was the presiding priest. He was dressed in a green chasuble. There were multiple nuns in the back of the church wearing black. I believe the Knights of Columbus were there, along with other lay people. The priest was calling peoples' names, to give them gifts and accolades for their good works on earth. While they were receiving their gifts, I saw myself step outside the church. As I walked through the front door, I saw the Son of Man with great power in the clear sky. He had short, dark hair. About thirty seconds later, I also saw his mother, Mary. She appeared above Him, dressed in a white robe and holding the infant Jesus.

There was also a ladder with six steps and two ropes suspended in the air, leading to Jesus. I called the people that were inside the church to come out, and I said to them, "It's Jesus"! They came outside and witnessed the Son of Man and his Blessed Mother in the sky. It was at this moment that I began to awake. Brothers and sisters, I want to let you know that our Savior's coming is near. It is time to pray. It is time to prepare ourselves to welcome Him.

SOURCES

www.Zo.Utexas.edu

www.nationsonline.org

Scripture quotations marked NJB are from the New Jerusalem Bible, copyright 1985 by Darton, Longman & Todd, Ltd. and Doubleday, a division of Random House, Inc. Reprinted by permission.

Scripture quotations marked NIV are from the the Holy Bible, New International Version, NIV, copyright 1973, 1978, 1984, 2011 by Biblica, Inc. Used by permission. All rights reserved worldwide.

Contemporary English Version
Copyright 1995 American Bible Society. All rights reserved.

Scriptures from the King James Version.

Cover from Shutterstock.com.

Printed in the United States
By Bookmasters